SCHOLASTIC

100 LITERACY HOMEWORK

RENEWED PRIMARY FRAMEWORK

100 LITERACY HOMEWORK ACTIVITIES

SCOTTISH PRIMARY 3

YEAR 2

D1421803

Credits

Author
Wendy Jolliffe, Kathleen Taylor
and David Waugh

Updated by
Kathleen Taylor

Series consultant
Pam Dowson

Series editor
Tracy Kewley

Development editor
Rachel Mackinnon

Assistant editor
Vicky Butt

Illustrations
Peter Smith/Beehive Illustration
Theresa Tibbetts/Beehive Illustration
and Garry Davies

Book layout
Macmillan Publishing Solutions

Mixed Sources
Product group from well-managed
forests and other controlled sources
www.fsc.org Cert no. TT-COC-002769
© 1996 Forest Stewardship Council
FSC

Text © 2001, 2009, Wendy Jolliffe,
Kathleen Taylor and David Waugh
© 2009 Scholastic Ltd

Designed using Adobe InDesign

Published by Scholastic Ltd
Villiers House
Clarendon Avenue
Leamington Spa
Warwickshire CV32 5PR

www.scholastic.co.uk

Printed by Bell and Bain Ltd, Glasgow

1 2 3 4 5 6 7 8 9   9 0 1 2 3 4 5 6 7 8

British Library Cataloguing-in-Publication Data
A catalogue record for this book is available from the British Library.

ISBN 978-1407-10116-3

The rights of Wendy Jolliffe, Kathleen Taylor and David Waugh to be identified
as the authors of this work have been asserted by them in accordance with the
Copyright, Designs and Patents Act 1988.

Extracts from the Primary National Strategy's *Primary Framework for
Literacy* (2006) http://nationalstrategies.standards.dcsf.gov.uk/primary/
primaryframework/ © Crown copyright. Reproduced under the terms of the Click
Use Licence.

Due to the nature of the web, we cannot guarantee the content or links of any
site mentioned. We strongly recommend that teachers check websites before
using them in the classroom.

Acknowledgements
The publishers gratefully acknowledge permission to reproduce the following
copyright material:

Curtis Brown for the use of 'Winter Morning' by Ogden Nash from *Collected
Poems* by Ogden Nash © 1962, Ogden Nash (1962, Little Brown). **Marian
Reiner Literary Agency** on behalf of the Boulder Public Library Foundation
Inc. for the use of the poem 'Noses' by Aileen Fisher from *Up the Windy Hill* by
Aileen Fisher © 1953, 1981 Aileen Fisher (1953, Aberlard-Schuman). **Dee Reid**
for the use of an extract from *Sack and the Jeanstalk* by Dee Reid © 1992, Dee
Reid (1992, Philograph Publications Limited).

Every effort has been made to trace copyright holders for the works reproduced
in this book, and the publishers apologise for any inadvertent omissions.

CONTENTS

INTRODUCTION
100 Literacy Homework Activities: Year 2

About the series

The *100 Literacy Homework Activities* series provides easy-to-use, photocopiable homework sheets for Key Stage 1 and 2 children. Each book in the series contains 100 homework activities that can be embedded into any school homework programme. Each activity sheet provides instructions for the child and a brief note to the helper, stating simply and clearly its purpose and suggesting support and/or further challenge to offer the child. The activities are clearly linked to the renewed Primary Framework for literacy and are organised by Block (Narrative, Non-fiction, Poetry), then by Unit.

Core skills activities

At the end of each unit, you will find a number of 'Core skills' activities, designed to support the development of key literacy skills such as word recognition (Years 1 and 2 only), word structure and spelling, and sentence structure and punctuation. Some of the Core skills activities are linked to the content of the units; others are intended to be used for discrete teaching and can be used at any time.

Teachers' notes

The teachers' notes starting on page 8 provide further information about each activity, with notes on setting the homework, differentiation and follow-up work. The Narrative/Non-fiction/Poetry objectives on the teachers' notes show how activities are linked to the Unit plans, while the reference grid on page 6 shows how the objectives from strands 1 to 12 of the Framework are covered in the book. Links to the Scottish curriculum are provided on the Scholastic website (see page 7).

Using the resources

The best way to use these homework resources is to use them flexibly, integrating them with a series of literacy sessions over a number of days. At primary level, homework should be about 'consolidating and reinforcing skills and understanding, particularly in literacy and numeracy' (Department for Children, Schools and Families: Homework Guidelines). Although the homework sheets can be used to support assessment, their main purpose is to reinforce and extend literacy work carried out in class or to help children prepare for upcoming work.

Supporting your helpers

It is vital that parents or carers understand what you are trying to achieve with homework. As well as the 'Dear helper' notes on each homework sheet, there is a homework diary on page 5 which can be photocopied and sent home with the homework. Multiple copies of these can be fastened together to make a longer term homework record. Discuss with parents/carers what is meant by 'help'. Legitimate help will include sharing the reading of texts, helping to clarify problems, discussing possible answers and so on, but at some stage the child should be left to do his or her best. Tell parents/carers how much time you expect the child to spend on homework. If, after that time, a child is stuck, or has not finished, they should not be forced to continue. Ask parents/carers to write a brief explanation and say that you will give extra help the next day. If children are succeeding with a task and need more time, this can be allowed – but bear in mind that children need a varied and balanced home life!

Using the activities with *100 Literacy Framework Lessons*

Links have been provided on the teachers' notes for those who wish to use the homework activities with the corresponding *100 Literacy Framework Lessons* book. The teachers' notes show if and where a homework task might fit within the context of the appropriate *100 Literacy Framework Lessons* Unit.

Homework diary

Name of activity and date sent home	Helper's comments	Child's comments		Teacher's comments
		Did you like this? Draw a face. 😊 a lot 😐 a little 😞 not much	**How much did you learn?** Draw a face. 😊 a lot 😐 a little 😞 not much	

Framework objectives

Objectives	Supporting activities (page numbers)
Strand 1: Speaking	
Speak with clarity and use appropriate intonation when reading and reciting texts.	40, 46, 54, 110, 111, 116, 118, 125
Tell real and imagined stories using the conventions of familiar story language.	29, 63
Explain ideas and processes using imaginative and adventurous vocabulary and non-verbal gestures to support communication.	52, 69, 81, 82, 84, 99, 113, 119, 123
Strand 2: Listening and responding	
Listen to others in class, ask relevant questions and follow instructions.	
Listen to talk by an adult, remember some specific points and identify what they have learned.	
Respond to presentations by describing characters, repeating some highlights and commenting constructively.	
Strand 3: Group discussion and interaction	
Ensure that everyone contributes, allocate tasks, and consider alternatives and reach agreement.	
Work effectively in groups by ensuring that each group member takes a turn challenging, supporting and moving on.	
Listen to each other's views and preferences, agree the next steps to take and identify contributions by each group member.	
Strand 4: Drama	
Adopt appropriate roles in small or large groups and consider alternative courses of action.	
Present part of traditional stories, their own stories or work from different parts of the curriculum for members of their own class.	
Consider how mood or atmosphere are created in live or recorded performance.	
Strand 5: Word recognition: decoding (reading) and encoding (spelling)	
Read independently and with increasing fluency longer and less familiar texts.	32, 40, 45, 46, 60, 62, 69, 70, 71, 85, 71, 91, 96, 99, 100, 101, 103, 104
Spell with increasing accuracy and confidence, drawing on word recognition and knowledge of word structure, and spelling patterns.	35, 38, 67, 76, 77, 78, 86, 87, 98, 106, 108, 115, 117, 121, 127
Know how to tackle unfamiliar words which are not completely decodable.	35, 70, 77, 85, 91, 100, 106, 109, 115
Read and spell less common alternative graphemes including trigraphs.	87, 109, 121
Read high and medium frequency words independently and automatically.	38, 78, 114, 125
Strand 6: Word structure and spelling	
Spell with increasing accuracy and confidence, drawing on word recognition and knowledge of word structure, and spelling patterns including common inflections and use of double letters.	35, 38, 67, 76, 77, 78, 86, 87, 98, 106, 108, 115, 117, 121, 127

Framework objectives

Objectives	Supporting activities (page numbers)
Strand 6: Word structure and spelling (cont.)	
Read and spell less common alternative graphemes including trigraphs.	87, 109, 121
Strand 7: Understanding and interpreting texts	
Draw together ideas and information from across a whole text, using simple signposts in the text.	28, 30, 31, 51, 68, 71, 99, 104
Give some reasons for why things happen or characters change.	28, 30, 41, 42, 43, 44, 52, 53, 55, 59, 60
Explain organisational features of texts, including alphabetical order, layout, diagrams, captions, hyperlinks and bullet points.	70, 71, 74, 79, 80, 83, 88, 89, 90, 92, 93, 95, 99, 102, 103
Use syntax and context to build their store of vocabulary when reading for meaning.	35, 48, 49, 51, 56, 66, 68, 70, 71, 75, 85, 88, 90, 94, 104
Explore how particular words are used, including words and expressions with similar meanings.	56, 62, 126
Strand 8: Engaging and responding to texts	
Read whole books on their own, choosing and justifying selections.	
Engage with books through exploring and enacting interpretations.	29, 36, 54, 97
Explain their reactions to texts, commenting on important aspects.	50, 52, 100, 101, 110, 111, 116, 117, 118, 122, 123
Strand 9: Creating and shaping texts	
Draw on knowledge and experience of texts in deciding and planning what and how to write.	32, 33, 34, 55, 64, 84, 105
Sustain form in narrative, including use of person and time.	29, 32, 33, 39, 45, 57, 58, 64
Maintain consistency in non-narrative, including purpose and tense.	83, 112, 125
Make adventurous word and language choices appropriate to style and purpose of text.	43, 110, 112, 113, 119, 122, 124, 126
Select from different presentational features to suit particular writing purposes on paper and on screen.	83, 113
Strand 10: Text structure and organisation	
Use planning to establish clear sections for writing.	34, 61, 64, 73, 74, 75, 84, 102, 103, 105, 113
Use appropriate language to make sections hang together.	62, 63, 72, 73
Strand 11: Sentence structure and punctuation	
Write simple and compound sentences and begin to use subordination in relation to time and reason.	31, 62, 73, 75
Compose sentences using tense consistently (present and past).	37, 45, 58
Use question marks, and use commas to separate items in a list.	47, 73, 96, 97, 107, 120
Links to the Scottish curriculum can be found at www.scholastic.co.uk/literacyhomework/y2 (click on Free resources)	

Narrative – Unit 1 Stories with familiar settings

Page 28 Lost on the beach
Narrative objective: To read stories focusing on the sequence of events.
Setting the homework: Explain that the children are being given the first part of a story. They should read it with their helpers and talk about the order in which events take place. They can then talk about what might happen next in the story.
Differentiation: It should be emphasised that everyone should read the story with their helper but that some children may wish to read it independently as well.
Back at school: Discuss the story with the children. You may wish to use the homework as a starting point for extended writing in which the children complete the story.
Link to *100 Literacy Framework Lessons Y2*: NU1, Sequence 1, Phase 1: sequencing the parts of a story.

Page 29 It was only yesterday
Narrative objective: To retell stories focusing on the sequence of events.
Setting the homework: Explain to the children that they will be reading a story and then retelling it to a parent or helper, making sure it is in the past, as if the story happened yesterday.
Back at school: Choose one or two children who are willing to tell the story, as if it happened yesterday, to the whole class. You may, in addition, like to ask some children to record their stories.

Page 30 Helping a friend
Narrative objective: To review stories and describe what a character does.
Setting the homework: Tell the children to read the story with their helper so that together they can explore, through the questions, the way that the character of David is revealed.
Differentiation: Questions 1 and 2 elicit responses at a literal level that all of the children should be able to do. Questions 3, 4, 5 and 6 demand a greater level of understanding including inferential interpretation. Some children will need more support with these questions.
Back at school: Organise the children in pairs. Give them the same scenario but say that they are the story characters. Ask them to consider what their own responses would be. Follow on by asking them how their responses compared to David's.
Link to *100 Literacy Framework Lessons Y2*: NU1, Sequence 1, Phase 2: exploring how characters have different points of view.

Page 31 The school trip
Narrative objective: To review stories and describe what a character does.
Setting the homework: Ask the children to read the extract carefully with their helper and then write answers to the questions, remembering to write in full sentences. The activity is linked to the one on page 32 and the two sheets could be used for consecutive homework tasks.
Back at school: Read the story together and ask different children to provide answers to the questions.

Page 32 The school trip – how does it end?
Narrative objective: To make predictions about characters' actions and the sequence of events.
Setting the homework: Tell the children that they will be reading a story about a school trip and writing their own ending about what happens. The activity is linked to the one on page 31 and the two sheets could be used for consecutive homework tasks.
Differentiation: Less confident learners could be provided with a series of blank frames on a piece of paper and draw their own ending in the form of a cartoon strip. Encourage them to write a simple caption to accompany each picture.
Back at school: Ask different children to share their endings to the story and see how they compare.

www.scholastic.co.uk

Page 33 Missing mouse

Narrative objective: To make predictions about characters' actions and the sequence of events.
Setting the homework: Read the story with the children and explain that they will be writing an ending for it. You may wish to discuss possibilities in order to give them some ideas, but emphasise that they should work out their own endings.
Differentiation: Helpers of less confident learners could be encouraged to act as scribes for their children. Alternatively, the children may be asked to read with their parents and then make notes which can be turned into a story at school with the help of an adult or as a whole-class shared writing activity.
Back at school: Share the children's endings. Using the notes from some of the less-confident learners, do a shared writing activity to write an ending as a class.
Link to *100 Literacy Framework Lessons Y2*: NU1, Sequence 2, Phase 1: predicting character action.

Page 34 What happened and when?

Narrative objective: To plan the structure of a story.
Setting the homework: Explain that the children will be using a framework to help them to write a story with their helpers.
Differentiation: Less confident learners may need help at school with reading words such as *suddenly* and *hardly*.
Back at school: Ask the children to read their stories aloud. Discuss the way in which some words and phrases show us that time has moved on in a story.
Link to *100 Literacy Framework Lessons Y2*: NU1, Sequence 2, Phase 2: story planning.

Page 35 At the seaside – Core skills

Objective: To use syntax and context to build their vocabulary when reading for meaning.
Setting the homework: Explain to the children that they will be learning some words related to being at the seaside. The task involves matching words to pictures.
Differentiation: Some children may be asked to play the game with fewer words than others. More confident learners could be asked to add new words and pictures related to the seaside.
Back at school: As a quick assessment of whether all the children have been able to complete this activity, prepare a set of word cards that have seaside vocabulary. Show these to the children and ask them to read them to you.

Page 36 What's black and white and read all over? – Core skills

Objective: To speak with clarity and intonation when reading and reciting texts.
Setting the homework: Talk to the children about the purpose of speech marks and show them an example of dialogue. Explain that they will need to look for speech marks in a short story to help them with the homework task. Read the text with the class.
Differentiation: Any children whom you feel may find the text difficult could be provided with simpler dialogue or could be asked to use a page from their reading books as the basis for the activity.
Back at school: As a quick assessment of whether all the children have been able to complete this activity, look at an enlarged example of dialogue and ask them to read only the spoken words aloud. You could follow this up further in group reading, with children taking turns to read by being assigned characters whose speech they should read.

Page 37 In the past – Core skills

Objective: To compose sentences using tense consistently.
Setting the homework: Explain to the children that they will need to rewrite sentences that are in the present tense (happening now) into the past tense (happened before). You may like to model the example given on the sheet.
Differentiation: Less confident learners could be encouraged to say their sentences aloud, preceding each sentence with *Yesterday...*
Back at school: Discuss examples of sentences in the past tense.

Page 38 Words we use a lot – Core skills

Objective: To read high and medium frequency words independently and automatically.
Setting the homework: Provide the children with a piece of text appropriate to their reading level and explain that they will be trying to find as many as possible of the words listed on their sheets. For example, give them the story 'Lost on the beach' on page 28.
Differentiation: Provide different pieces of text for children according to their ability levels. More confident learners could use newspapers or be asked to find their own texts.
Back at school: Invite the children to share some of the sentences they have identified containing high frequency words. Revise the spelling of these words.

Narrative – Unit 2 Traditional stories

Page 39 Sack and the Jeanstalk

Narrative objective: To explore alternative versions of traditional stories.
Setting the homework: Explain to the children that they will be reading an extract from a funny version of 'Jack and the Beanstalk'. They will need to find which words are wrong, for example *Once upon a **line**...*, and underline all those words. Then they should look carefully at the pictures of the beginning, middle and end of the correct story, and write sentences to fit each picture.
Back at school: Discuss the wrong words that the children have identified in 'Sack and the Jeanstalk', then invite them to read out their sentences relating to the original story. Display enlarged copies of the pictures on the homework sheet together with the sentences that the children have written.

Page 40 Troll's noisy problem

Narrative objective: To read and compare alternative versions of traditional stories.
Setting the homework: Tell the children that the story 'Troll's noisy problem' is a different version of 'The Three Billy Goats Gruff' told from the Troll's point of view. Say that it would be useful to access the online version of the traditional tale on the website http://ngfl. northumberland.gov.uk/english/goats/billygoatsgruff.html
Back at school: Organise the children into small groups and ask them to discuss how other traditional stories might be changed in a similar way. For example, they could tell the story of 'Jack and the Beanstalk' from the Giant's point of view.
Link to *100 Literacy Framework Lessons Y2*: NU2, Phase 2: reversing the roles of good and bad characters.

Page 41 Say and do

Narrative objective: To discuss opposing characters from a narrative.
Setting the homework: Tell the children that they will use the pictures on the homework sheet, together with what is being said, to help them talk about why and how we know a character is good or bad.
Back at school: Extend the activity through group discussion. Organise for small groups to further explain how they came to their decisions by referring to evidence in the pictures and what is said.

Page 42 From good to bad

Narrative objective: To compose dialogue for characters.
Setting the homework: Explain to the children that they are going to change Red Riding Hood and Cinderella from being kind, helpful and polite characters into characters who are not. They are going to achieve this by changing the kind and helpful things they say into cruel and unhelpful things.
Differentiation: Some children will need help in scribing their ideas.
Back at school: Provide opportunities for children to draw or paint their new characters capturing the cruel, unkind and impolite characteristics. Some children could draw and paint the original kind characters.
Link to *100 Literacy Framework Lessons Y2*: NU2, Phase 2, Day 2: creating new dialogue for characters.

Page 43 Two different people?
Narrative objective: To explore how characters behave if their roles are exchanged.
Setting the homework: Explain that we need to choose our words carefully if we are to provide accurate descriptions of people. Show some examples of descriptions of people that could be changed dramatically if one or two words were altered.
Differentiation: The most confident children could be asked to write their own contrasting character profiles.
Back at school: Enlarge or copy out some examples of children's work and discuss the antonyms they have used. If any children have written their own profiles, look at these with the class and discuss the antonyms that have been used.
Link to *100 Literacy Framework Lessons Y2*: NU2, Phase 2: reversing the roles of good and bad characters.

Page 44 What's in a picture?
Narrative objective: To discuss how images can convey information to a reader.
Setting the homework: Tell the children that pictures in a story can help to tell you what the characters are like and what is happening in a story. Say that it would be useful to access the online version of the traditional tale on the website www.bbc.co.uk/cbeebies/stories (select Cinderella from the A to Z menu). Ask the children to say what each picture on the homework sheet represents.
Differentiation: Ask more confident learners to think of other objects in the 'Cinderella' story that could represent either the way a character behaves or feels, or an event in the story.
Back at school: Extend the differentiated task so that all of the children can consider the meaning conveyed in images from the story such as the mice, the cat, the glass slipper and the Fairy Godmother.
Link to *100 Literacy Framework Lessons Y2*: NU2, Phase 3: how images can portray information to the reader.

Page 45 Birthday ball
Narrative objective: To use temporal connectives to write a story.
Setting the homework: Read the beginning of the story to the children pointing out the connecting words. Tell them that they are going to continue to write the story in their own words. Remind the children of the useful words they have been using to connect information within a sentence and to join some sentences together.
Differentiation: Some children will need to rehearse telling the story to their helper and this should be encouraged as part of setting the homework.
Back at school: Provide opportunities for children to tell their stories to one another in small groups.
Link to *100 Literacy Framework Lessons Y2*: NU2, Phase 2: work on 'Cinderella' and the use of temporal connectives.

Page 46 Jill and Jack – Core skills
Objective: To revise the use of capital letters.
Setting the homework: Explain that the children have a story to read and that they will need to look closely at the capital letters in the story and decide why each is used.
Differentiation: More confident learners might be given a more challenging text. Less confident learners may need a simpler text and could be given a copy of a page of their school reading book.
Back at school: Look at an enlarged version of the text with the children and ask them to take turns to explain the reason for each capital letter.

Page 47 Talking to the giant – Core skills
Objective: To use question marks and exclamation marks.
Setting the homework: Explain to the children that they need to add question marks and exclamation marks to the speech bubbles from the story of 'Jack and the Beanstalk'. They will also need to add full stops.
Differentiation: Less confident learners may need their helpers to read the speech with correct intonation to help them decide what punctuation to use.
Back at school: Discuss the punctuation required for these examples. You could enlarge the speech bubbles to form part of a display on 'Jack and the Beanstalk'.

Page 48 Opposites – Core skills
Objective: To use syntax to build their store of vocabulary when reading for meaning.
Setting the homework: Explain that there are two lists on the homework sheet and that the children need to draw lines to link the words that are opposites of each other. Use the word 'antonym' if appropriate. Provide an example on the board.
Differentiation: More confident learners could be asked to produce further lists of opposites for each other to attempt at school.
Back at school: Make a list on the board of some of the additional opposites that children found and ask the class to match the pairs. Talk about spellings and about any prefixes that are used to create opposites.

Page 49 Find the opposite – Core skills
Objective: To use syntax to build their store of vocabulary when reading for meaning.
Setting the homework: Explain that the homework sheet has a list of words, each of which has at least one opposite. Provide a few examples on the board and ask children to consider possible opposites. Talk about the use of prefixes such as 'un-' and 'dis-' which may be used to create some opposites. Use the word 'antonym' if appropriate.
Differentiation: More confident learners could be asked to use dictionaries to find examples of words that begin with 'un-' and 'dis-' and to write some of them in a list. You will need to talk about other words that begin with 'un-' and 'dis-' in which 'un-' and 'dis-' are not prefixes for opposites (for example, *united, university, dish, disgust*).
Back at school: Look at some of the examples of opposites that the children have found and focus on those that have the prefixes 'un-' or 'dis-'. Provide further examples and see if the children have understood how to add a prefix to make a negative.

Narrative – Unit 3 Different stories by the same author

Page 50 My opinion
Narrative objective: To express personal responses to an author.
Setting the homework: Tell the children that they are to choose a book they have read recently and use the questions on the homework sheet to help them express their opinion about the story. Explain the need for the children to consider the questions carefully so that their answers are well reasoned.
Differentiation: The questions on the homework sheet afford different levels of challenge.
Back at school: In a whole-class lesson, ask confident children to model how to identify the most important aspects that have informed their opinion.
Link to *100 Literacy Framework Lessons Y2*: NU3, Phase 1: reviewing stories.

Page 51 About the author
Narrative objective: To find out interesting information about an author.
Setting the homework: Refer to the class library or the books the children are reading to set the scene for the children to think about their favourite authors. Tell them that they are going to find out information about their favourite author using the internet.
Differentiation: All of the children should be able to do this task. Some children will require extra support including help with vocabulary that describes specific genres. Some examples of genres are given on the homework sheet.
Back at school: Establish discussion groups where children listen to each other's views and preferences.
Link to *100 Literacy Framework Lessons Y2*: NU3, Phase 1: using the internet to find out about an author.

Page 52 Pen portrait

Narrative objective: To explore characterisation in an author's books.

Setting the homework: Remind the children how authors describe characters through what they say, do and think and what others say, do and think about them and that this is the evidence that tells you about the character. Refer to the instructions on the homework sheet. Emphasise the need for the helper to support the child in interpreting evidence from the text in order to provide a collection of words and phrases that describe the character.

Back at school: Select extracts containing dialogue from the some of the books the children have chosen so that they can enact their favourite characters. This will deepen their interpretation of the character.

Link to *100 Literacy Framework Lessons Y2*: NU3, Phase 2: using evidence from a text to talk about character.

Page 53 Character sketches

Narrative objective: To explore character by gathering evidence from the text.

Setting the homework: Explain that the homework sheet has descriptions of characters and pictures of them but that the pictures and descriptions need to be sorted out so that they match. Talk about the use of adjectives to describe characters and encourage the children to use them when they are writing their own character sketches.

Differentiation: More confident learners may be asked to write more character sketches and should be encouraged to look for descriptions in story books.

Back at school: Ask the children to read aloud some of their character sketches. Write some of the adjectives they use on the board and discuss their meanings and spellings.

Page 54 In character

Narrative objective: To explore character by gathering evidence from the text.

Setting the homework: Explain to the children that they and their helpers are going to become characters in a story by reading dialogue. They can take turns in being the characters to explore the nature of character A and character B.

Back at school: Choose a confident pair of children to enact the dialogue. Then choose two other children to respond to the presentations by describing the characters and identifying aspects of the dialogue that reveal the nature of the characters.

Page 55 Invent a character

Narrative objective: To create a character upon which to base a story.

Setting the homework: Refer to the homework sheet to tell the children what they have to do. Emphasise why choosing the right name is important for the story to feel right and that they might have to change the name of the main character as they make decisions about what the character is like and what might happen.

Back at school: Organise the children in pairs so that they can tell each other their story. Set the children the task of responding constructively to each other's story.

Page 56 Stop throwing paint! – Core skills

Objective: To use syntax and context to build their store of vocabulary when reading for meaning.

Setting the homework: Explain to the children that they will be reading a piece of dialogue and that they will need to read it carefully to decide how each speaker might have said the words that are spoken.

Differentiation: Read the dialogue with children who may need to become familiar with the vocabulary before taking the text home. Some children may need to be given a simpler text to work on.

Back at school: Talk about the verbs that the children ascribed to each speaker and then look at further examples of such verbs in texts that are familiar to the children.

Page 57 Who said that? – Core skills
Objective: To sustain form in narrative including use of time.
Setting the homework: Show the children some examples of verbs that accompany speech from the current class story book and talk about the way they tend to be written in the past tense. Explain that the children will be looking at similar verbs and will need to write them in the correct tense.
Differentiation: Ask more confident learners to use their reading books to find other examples of verbs used to describe speech.
Back at school: Look at further examples of verbs and, with the children's help, write these in both the present and past tenses.

Page 58 Matching past and present – Core skills
Objective: To compose sentences using tense consistently (present and past).
Setting the homework: Explain to the children that they will need to match the verbs (action words) in the present tense (happening now) with the corresponding ones in the past tense (happened before). You may like to model the example given on the homework sheet.
Differentiation: Less confident learners may be encouraged to put the words into sentences, saying their sentences aloud and preceding each appropriately with *Today...* and *Yesterday...* Additionally, you may wish to limit the number of words for less confident learners.
Back at school: Display examples of words in the past tense and discuss them. For instance, you could make use of a puppet who keeps getting the words in the past tense wrong and the children have to correct him (such as *I feeled ill, I runned fast* and so on).

Narrative – Unit 4 Extended stories/significant authors

Page 59 What happens next?
Narrative objective: To make predictions at key moments in the story.
Setting the homework: Emphasise the importance of the children's discussion with their helper in this activity.
Differentiation: Some children will need more support from their helper to interpret the text and make predictions about what might happen.
Back at school: During guided reading, focus on predicting what might happen next.
Link to *100 Literacy Framework Lessons Y2*: NU4, Phase 1: making predictions about a story.

Page 60 What will Francis do?
Narrative objective: To make predictions at key moments in the story.
Setting the homework: Emphasise the importance of the children's discussion with their helper in this activity.
Differentiation: Some children will need support. Give them the scenario but say that it is happening to them. Ask: *What would you do?* Then draw them back to the text to decide what Francis would do.
Back at school: Organise the children into groups ensuring that each group has a selection of stories about Francis where the outcomes are different. Tell the children to discuss the outcomes and give reasons why they think some are more plausible than others.
Link to *100 Literacy Framework Lessons Y2*: NU4, Phase 1: making predictions and discussing the way characters develop.

Page 61 Beginnings and endings
Narrative objective: To evaluate story language by sorting beginnings and endings of stories.
Setting the homework: Explain to the children that the beginning of a story needs to have a sense of anticipation so that one wants to read on and that the end of a story needs to provide a satisfying feeling that everything has been drawn together. Tell the children to consider this when sorting out the list of beginnings and endings.
Differentiation: Some children could be asked to provide reasons for their choices.
Back at school: As a whole-class lesson, examine why some of the examples from the list could be used either as a beginning or an ending. Encourage the children to justify their selections.

Page 62 Family holiday
Narrative objective: To use temporal connectives in a story.
Setting the homework: Explain to the children that they have a choice of linking words – but that some are better than others – to use to link information in the story.
Differentiation: All of the children will need support in reading the story and in choosing the most appropriate linking word or phrases. Some children will benefit from being shown the process of reading the sentence with each of the possible choices before deciding which is best.
Back at school: Organise the children into small groups of about four so that they can talk about the suitability of the linking words and phrases that have been used in the completed story. Encourage the children to comment, giving reasons for their preferences.
Link to *100 Literacy Framework Lessons Y2***:** NU4, Phase 2: adding temporal connectives to a story.

Page 63 Connect the pictures
Narrative objective: To use temporal connectives in a story.
Setting the homework: Tell the children that they are going to write a story from the pictures on the homework sheet and that they have been given some useful connective words and phrases to help them link the events together.
Back at school: Organise the children into pairs where they swap stories so that each can underline the connecting words and phrases that their partner has used.
Link to *100 Literacy Framework Lessons Y2***:** NU4, Phase 2: adding temporal connectives to a story.

Page 64 Aladdin's adventure
Narrative objective: To plan a story with a logical sequence of events.
Setting the homework: Tell the children that by using their imagination they are going to construct a story using the picture cards as prompts to help them follow the set plot.
Differentiation: All of the children will need support through discussion with their helper to construct the story. Some will need to be reminded of the story plot as they construct their story.
Back at school: Choose children to explain how a picture card helped them to form an idea for their story.

Page 65 Choose the right word – Core skills
Objective: To use syntax and context to build a store of vocabulary when reading for meaning.
Setting the homework: Show the children a few examples of sentences with words missing and ask them to suggest words which would complete them. Talk about using the text before and after a missing word to help determine what the word might be.
Differentiation: Some children could be given the sentences to complete without having a selection of words provided.
Back at school: Try further examples with the whole class or with groups of children to ascertain if they are able to make use of semantic and syntactic clues.

Page 66 Find the capitals – Core skills
Objective: To revise the use of capital letters.
Setting the homework: Explain that the children will need to use their reading books and other texts to find capital letters and then classify them according to the reasons for their usage.
Differentiation: Ensure that the children use texts that are appropriate to their reading levels.
Back at school: Make a class chart similar to that on the homework sheet and, using a piece of text currently being used for shared reading, fill in the chart and display it next to the text.

Page 67 Find the compound words – Core skills
Objective: To identify compound words and their component parts.
Setting the homework: Explain to the children that the passage that they have been given includes several compound words. You may wish to tell them exactly how many there are (there are 13 different words – the word *playground* is repeated). Show them some examples of compound words and ask them to divide the words into their constituent parts.
Differentiation: You may wish to underline some of the words to help less confident learners. More confident learners could be given a more extensive piece to work on.
Back at school: Look at an enlarged version of the text with the children and ask them to identify and then split the compound words. Go on to provide further examples then ask them to do the same with those words.

Non-fiction – Unit 1 Instructions

Page 68 Simon says!
Non-fiction objective: To practise following instructions.
Setting the homework: Ensure that children know their left and right.
Differentiation: Less confident learners may benefit from trying out similar activities in school before attempting the homework. More confident learners could add further instruction cards to enhance the game.
Back at school: Ask the children to follow simple written instructions as a class or in ability groups. You could do this by writing a series of instructions similar to those in the homework activity on the board and then pointing to them randomly and asking the children to follow them.
Link to *100 Literacy Framework Lessons Y2*: NFU1, Sequence 1, Phase 2: playing 'Simon says'.

Page 69 Stick in the mud
Non-fiction objective: To practise giving oral instructions.
Setting the homework: Explain that the game featured on the homework sheet needs at least three players and preferably more. Some children might like to get together (with parents' or helpers' permission) and read the instructions and then play the game. Ask the children to find out some of the rhymes their parents used to use to determine who would go first in a game.
Back at school: Ask the children how effective the instructions were and find out if some people played the game in different ways. Ask the children about the rhymes their parents used to use for games and write some of these on the board to model poetry writing for the children.
Link to *100 Literacy Framework Lessons Y2*: NFU1, Sequence 1, Phases 2 and 3: giving oral instructions.

Page 70 Making a pancake
Non-fiction objective: To explore the organisational feature of instructions.
Setting the homework: Explain what *utensils* and *ingredients* are. If possible, provide some examples of recipes that have items listed separately.
Differentiation: Some children may need to be given help in advance with some of the words that appear in the recipe. This could form part of a guided reading session in which you work with a group and look at similar recipes.
Back at school: Talk with the children about utensils and ingredients. Show further examples of recipes and ask them to tell you which items are utensils and which ingredients.
Link to *100 Literacy Framework Lessons Y2*: NFU1, Sequence 2, Phases 1 and 2: examining features of instructions.

Page 71 Reading instructions
Non-fiction objective: To read and follow simple instructions.
Setting the homework: Talk with the children about paper aeroplanes and ensure that everyone understands what they are.
Differentiation: Less confident learners may need to become familiarised with some of the vocabulary in the instructions before attempting the homework.
Back at school: Ask the children to bring in their paper aeroplanes, and talk with them about the quality of the instructions.

Page 72 Cleaning your teeth
Non-fiction objective: To analyse language features of written instructions.
Setting the homework: Ensure that the children understand that link words (such as *first, next, after, before, when* and *finally*) help us to show sequence in texts.
Differentiation: More confident learners could be asked to change the beginnings of some of the sentences to include words such as *meanwhile* and *during*.
Back at school: Check that the children have understood the purpose of the linking words by doing some shared writing of instructions or a story.
Link to *100 Literacy Framework Lessons Y2*: NFU1, Sequence 2, Phases 1 and 2: examining features of instructions.

Page 73 Write your own instructions

Non-fiction objective: To write own instructions.

Setting the homework: Explain that the children will need to find instructions at home and that the following may be useful sources: recipe books, magazines, self-assembly models, do-it-yourself books, manuals for electrical goods.

Differentiation: Less confident learners will probably need parents or helpers to act as scribes when producing instructions.

Back at school: Show examples of the children's instructions and talk about the words that often begin instruction sentences. Write some of them on the board and discuss their meanings.

Link to *100 Literacy Framework Lessons Y2*: NFU1, Sequence 2, Phase 3: writing instructions.

Page 74 Hide and seek

Non-fiction objective: To write own instructions.

Setting the homework: Explain that you would like the children to make use of their knowledge of instructions to write their own instructions for a game. You may wish to show them how to write instructions that match illustrations.

Differentiation: Less confident learners may be asked to limit their instructions to words and phrases rather than complete sentences but, providing they have adequate support at home, they should be encouraged to work with their helpers to write complete sentences.

Back at school: Read some of the children's instructions aloud and ask the children to comment upon them and compare and contrast different versions.

Link to *100 Literacy Framework Lessons Y2*: NFU1, Sequence 2, Phase 3: writing instructions.

Page 75 Writing instructions

Non-fiction objective: To write and evaluate own instructions.

Setting the homework: Show some examples of instructions that are accompanied by illustrations and some that consist of illustrations alone. Self-assembly furniture packs are a good source.

Differentiation: Less confident learners could be asked to draw illustrations and limit written instructions to short phrases.

Back at school: Use some of the children's instructions in the classroom and ask others to attempt to follow them and make paper aeroplanes. Discuss the importance of clarity and precision.

Link to *100 Literacy Framework Lessons Y2*: NFU1, Sequence 2, Phase 3: writing and evaluating instructions.

Page 76 Making compound words – Core skills

Objective: To use syntax and context to build a store of vocabulary when reading for meaning.

Setting the homework: Provide a few examples of words that could be combined to make compound words and ask the class to suggest some possible combinations. Encourage the use of simple dictionaries to check the words that are produced.

Back at school: As a quick assessment of whether all the children have understood this activity, write on the board some words that could be used to make compound words. Ask the children to suggest pairs of words that could be joined to create compounds. You could divide the class into two teams and let each team take turns to come up with a word.

Page 77 How many syllables? – Core skills

Objective: To spell with increasing accuracy, drawing on knowledge of word structure.

Setting the homework: Practise, with the children, clapping syllables in familiar words and in their names. Explain that they are going to find words with different numbers of syllables.

Differentiation: Some children could be asked to find only one-, two- and three-syllable words, while others could be challenged to find words with five or more syllables.

Back at school: Ask individuals to clap their names and those of others.

Page 78 Matching syllables – Core skills
Objective: To spell with increasing accuracy, drawing on knowledge of word structure.
Setting the homework: Explain to the children that they will be playing a matching game based on syllables. You may wish to try the game with the whole class with a limited number of words.
Differentiation: The number and complexity of the words may be varied according to the ability levels of the children. You may wish to provide prepared sets of words for some.
Back at school: As a quick assessment of whether all the children have been able to complete this activity, write a series of words with one, two, three or four syllables on the board and ask the children to help you to sort them according to their numbers of syllables.

Non-fiction – Unit 2 Explanations

Page 79 Find out where
Non-fiction objective: To identify and use organisational features of explanation texts.
Setting the homework: Explain to the children that they will need to answer the questions on the homework sheet by looking at the index that is provided. Tell them that the index has been taken from a non-fiction book about pets. Make sure the children understand that they will have to think clearly about some of the questions, for example ask: *Which pet could be described as dangerous?*
Back at school: Using an enlarged copy of the index 'All about pets' on the homework sheet, ask different children to answer the questions.
Link to *100 Literacy Framework Lessons Y2*: Non-fiction Unit 2, Phase 1 – using an index.

Page 80 Make an index
Non-fiction objective: To construct an index.
Setting the homework: Explain that the children will need to first put the words into alphabetical order, then write the toys and page numbers to make their own index.
Differentiation: Children who are less secure in their knowledge of the alphabet may find an alphabet strip on a card helpful in order to sort the items alphabetically.
Back at school: Invite the children to show their indexes to the rest of the class. Encourage them to discuss how easy they found the task.

Page 81 How I do my shopping
Non-fiction objective: To organise stages of a process.
Setting the homework: Explain that the children will be given a sheet with boxes in which different stages of shopping at the supermarket are described. They will then have to read them carefully and place them in the correct order.
Differentiation: More confident learners could be asked to produce their own flowcharts for shopping.
Back at school: Ask the children to take turns to show their versions of the flowchart to the rest of the class. Make an enlarged flowchart for another process.

Page 82 How I made a bulb light up
Non-fiction objective: To investigate key features of explanation texts.
Setting the homework: This task should be used to complement science lessons on electricity. Tell the children that the sentences in the boxes explain how to make a bulb light up using just a battery, two wires and a bulb. Show the children how what is said at the end of one sentence links to the beginning of another.
Differentiation: Some children will need more help in reading the sentences because of the new science terminology they have been learning.
Back at school: Organise for a whole-class lesson. Provide a battery, two wires and a light bulb (light bulb holder if used) on a table for selected children to use to show and explain how to make a bulb light up.
Link to *100 Literacy Framework Lessons Y2*: NFU2, Phase 1: features of explanation texts.

Page 83 How I grew a bean

Non-fiction objective: To write own explanation text sequenced correctly.

Setting the homework: Demonstrate planting a bean to show the whole class how this is done. This could be linked to a science topic. Explain to the children that the homework sheet is to remind them of how to plant a bean and that they will need to think about how to help it grow in order to provide their explanations.

Differentiation: Some children will be able to imagine having grown the bean and provide an explanation of the whole process. Others may only draw from the actual experience of planting the bean.

Back in the class: Select and enlarge a child's homework sheet with their permission and involve that child in modelling how explanation text is constructed by pointing out the linking words and phrases.

Page 84 Make your own flowchart

Non-fiction objective: To construct a pictorial flowchart.

Setting the homework: Explain that the homework sheet has an example of a flowchart and that you would like the children to choose another process and create their own flowcharts.

Differentiation: The children could be encouraged to include more or fewer stages in their processes according to ability. Some children may need to confine their writing to simple words and phrases accompanied by sketches.

Back at school: Look at the children's flowcharts with the whole class and discuss them. Choose some good examples and enlarge them so that everyone may look at them together. Make a further flowchart with the whole class to check on the children's understanding.

Link to *100 Literacy Framework Lessons Y2*: NFU2, Phase 3: constructing flowcharts.

Page 85 Match the meaning – Core skills

Objective: To use syntax and context to build their store of vocabulary when reading for meaning.

Setting the homework: Explain to the children that they will be matching the words to the meanings on the homework sheet. They can refer to a dictionary if they wish.

Differentiation: Less confident learners could be provided with simpler words, or the number of words could be limited.

Back at school: Ask different children to share examples of synonyms. Alternatively, if you write some of the words on cards, together with synonyms, you could ask the children to hold up the cards and find a partner who has a word with the same meaning.

Page 86 Word sums – Core skills

Objective: To spell with increasing accuracy, drawing on knowledge of word structure.

Setting the homework: Explain to the children that they will be given a selection of compound words and be asked to split them into the words which go together to form them.

Differentiation: More confident learners could be provided with additional compound words and be asked to find others in their reading books and other texts.

Back at school: As a quick assessment of whether all the children have been able to complete this activity, write a series of compound words on the board and ask the class to help you to divide them into their constituent parts.

Page 87 Words within words (1) – Core skills

Objective: To spell with increasing accuracy and confidence, drawing on knowledge of word structure and spelling patterns.

Setting the homework: Explain to the children that they need to find words hidden inside the longer words. If possible, work through one example with the class.

Differentiation: This will largely be by outcome, according to the number of words children find. A similar word-finding activity, 'Words within words (2)', which may be more suitable for some children, appears on page 115.

Back at school: Display the number of words found, possibly by the classroom door so that parents and helpers can see the results!

Non-fiction – Unit 3 Information texts

Page 88 The language of books
Non-fiction objective: To investigate non-fiction books.
Setting the homework: Explain to the children that they will need to look closely at the picture of the book cover and the labels around it. They will then need to write what each of the words means. You might like to provide one example, such as *illustrator – the person who draws the illustrations or pictures in the book.*
Differentiation: You could extend this activity for more confident learners by asking them to look at a range of books at home or in the local library and compile a list of titles, authors, illustrators and so on.
Back at school: Prepare some large cards showing the terminology *title, illustrator, author, publisher, blurb, bar code* and *price*, and ask the children to help to label a Big Book for display in the classroom.

Page 89 Find the telephone number
Non-fiction objective: To use alphabetically ordered texts such as directories.
Setting the homework: Children will need access to a telephone directory (explain that they can find one in a public library if they do not have one at home). They will need to scan quickly for the correct alphabetical page and then look through for the specific name and initial. (The names included are very common and most of them should be found in most telephone directories, but you could adapt the sheet with names in your own local directory, if necessary.) Ensure the children understand that they should not phone any of the numbers they find.
Differentiation: For less confident learners, the number of names could be limited. Also, if the selection is restricted so that there is only one name for each initial letter, the task will be made easier.
Back at school: If you have one or two old telephone directories at school, ask the children to demonstrate finding a name in a directory.

Page 90 Cover story
Non-fiction objective: To close read text to find information.
Setting the homework: Explain that the children will be looking closely at illustrations of book covers and then completing information in a grid. Tell them that sometimes they will write the title and sometimes the information contained in the book. They can include what is written on the blurb, as well as adding to this to include other information that may be contained. For example, a book titled *Insects* could include information on types of insects as well as body parts and feeding habits.
Back at school: Invite the children to share the information about the books that they have inserted in the grid on the homework sheet. Encourage them to offer any extra ideas about the books' contents.

Page 91 Noting the facts
Non-fiction objective: To make simple notes from non-fiction texts.
Setting the homework: Explain to the children that they will be reading an extract about maiasaurs (a type of dinosaur) and will need to write notes in the grid. You may like to provide an example, such as *Size when fully grown – 9 metres long.*
Back at school: Ask selected children to share examples of notes they have made.
Link to *100 Literacy Framework Lessons Y2*: NFU3, Sequence 1, Phase 2: making notes from a text.

Page 92 Where does it belong?
Non-fiction objective: To create an alphabetically ordered text.
Setting the homework: Discuss catalogues with the children and tell them that they will be selecting words from the lists at the top of the homework sheet to write in the correct sections, remembering to use alphabetical order. You may need to explain the word *accessories.*
Back at school: The information on the completed homework sheets could form part of a class activity in which the children put together a catalogue comprising pages that they have made themselves.

Page 93 Write a dictionary page

Non-fiction objective: To create an alphabetically ordered dictionary.
Setting the homework: Explain to the children that the words and definitions are at the top of the page and that they need to write the words and the corresponding meanings in the grid. Remind them to make sure that they put the words in alphabetical order.
Back at school: Talk about the words and correct definitions. You could follow this up by making a class dictionary.
Link to *100 Literacy Framework Lessons Y2*: NFU3, Sequence 2, Phase 2: creating alphabetically ordered texts.

Page 94 It's a match! – Core skills

Objective: To use syntax and context to build a store of vocabulary when reading for meaning.
Setting the homework: Explain to the children that they will be making cards for a game to play with a helper. The game is a pairs game in which they have to match words to their meanings. The vocabulary included on the homework sheet is the same as that on the previous sheet (page 93).
Differentiation: You may like to include simpler words and definitions for less confident learners.
Back at school: Ask groups of children to play the game as an independent activity during a literacy lesson.

Page 95 Alphabetical order – Core skills

Objective: To explain organisational features of texts, including alphabetical order.
Setting the homework: Spend some time showing children how to use the second and third letters to determine alphabetical order when words have the same beginnings. You could use common irregular words for this activity or you could use names of children in the class.
Differentiation: You may wish to provide more confident learners with longer lists of words including some in which the first three letters are the same.
Back at school: Check children's ability to spell irregular words by holding an informal spelling quiz.

Page 96 Punctuate the passage – Core skills

Objective: To revise the use of the full stop and to use commas to separate items in a list.
Setting the homework: Ensure that the children know about the use and purpose of full stops and commas. Read a bit of the passage on the homework sheet, without pausing at all. Ask the children to identify what's wrong. Explain that they should read the passage with their helper and put in the punctuation that will help the reader to read and understand the passage.
Differentiation: Some children may need to work on only a portion of the text, or a simpler text altogether.
Back at school: Display a correctly punctuated copy of the passage and discuss with the children how the punctuation has helped both reading and understanding.

Page 97 The question mark challenge – Core skills

Objective: To use question marks.
Setting the homework: Explain to the children that they will be reading some text in which the question marks have been taken out. There are many questions in the story, so there are many question marks missing. Can they find where they should be and put them in?
Differentiation: Less confident learners may need help in reading the text. They could try sharing the reading with their helper, each taking a role.
Back at school: Enlarge a copy of the story for the children to punctuate.

Page 98 Adding '-ing' – Core skills

Objective: To spell with increasing accuracy, drawing on knowledge of word structure and spelling patterns.
Setting the homework: Revise the rules for adding '-ing' by using the explanation on the homework sheet.
Differentiation: Less confident learners may need to be reminded of the terminology ('verb', 'vowel', 'consonant') and the difference between long and short vowels.
Back at school: Display an enlarged version of the sheet and go over the words while the children check their own.

Non-fiction – Unit 4 Non-chronological reports

Page 99 Children's games
Non-fiction objective: To identify common features of a non-chronological report.
Setting the homework: Explain to the children that the homework task is linked to their current work on writing reports and linked to the Victorians in history. Tell the children that the questions focus on the report's structure, to help them learn more about how reports are organised.
Back at school: Provide opportunities for the children, working in pairs, to discuss other reports where they use questions similar to the ones on the homework sheet to judge the quality of the report.
Link to *100 Literacy Framework Lessons Y2*: NFU4, Phase 1: identifying features of non-chronological reports/work on the Victorians.

Page 100 Birds in our garden
Non-fiction objective: To evaluate the effectiveness of texts.
Setting the homework: Explain to the children that the 'Report on birds' may not be the best example of report writing. Tell them to use the 'success criteria grid' to begin judging the good and poor aspects of the report. Tell them to add any other success criteria they think of to the grid.
Differentiation: All of the children should use the success criteria given on the grid. Some children will be able to add their own success criteria.
Back at school: Extend this activity by asking the children to explain how they would improve the report in the areas that they have identified as poor.
Link to *100 Literacy Framework Lessons Y2*: NFU4, Phase 1, Days 3 and 4: evaluating non-chronological reports.

Page 101 In the city
Non-fiction objective: To evaluate the effectiveness of texts.
Setting the homework: Discuss with the children the success criteria used in judging a report. If necessary, refer to the success criteria grid in the homework activity 'Birds in our garden' (page 100). Explain that they are going to make a list of questions to ask another child about the report on the homework sheet called 'City living'.
Differentiation: Some children may need to be given the success criteria grid questions as a starting point for creating their own questions.
Back at school: Organise the children into pairs so that they can take turns in asking the questions they have posed about the text.
Link to *100 Literacy Framework Lessons Y2*: NFU4, Phase 1, Days 3 and 4: evaluating non-chronological reports.

Page 102 My travels
Non-fiction objective: To plan a non-chronological report using subheadings.
Setting the homework: Explain to the children that they will first need to write down all the places they have travelled to, how they have travelled and who they have travelled with in order to make a collection. Emphasise that the most important part of this task is grouping the information as this will form the sections of a book's contents page. You may wish to demonstrate this by collecting similar ideas on the theme of travelling or relevant class topic, followed by sorting these out into appropriately titled sections. Explain to the children that their journey to a local shop is just as relevant to this activity as a holiday overseas; similarly, travels on foot or bicycle are also just as important as travel by air.
Back at school: In a whole-class lesson, choose children to show and explain how they have grouped information for the contents page of their book about travels and compare with a real book (Big Book) and contents page.
Link to *100 Literacy Framework Lessons Y2*: NFU4, Phase 1, Days 3 and 4: evaluating non-chronological reports.

Page 103 Sports report

Non-fiction objective: To organise ideas under subheadings into a paragraph.

Setting the homework: Tell the children that they will need help in reading the 'Sports report'. Explain that they are going to make its appearance more interesting by adding headings and subheadings to highlight the various pieces of information. Encourage the children to be adventurous and creative with their headings to make them stand out.

Back at school: In a whole-class lesson, use the interactive whiteboard to show some of the tools available such as font type, size and colour in order to make the headings and subheadings stand out on the report to make its appearance more effective. Explain to the children what the terms 'font', 'bold' and so on mean.

Page 104 We need energy!

Non-fiction objective: To make simple notes from a text.

Setting the homework: This homework should follow a lesson in which you have modelled how to scan to pick out key points from text and make notes.

Differentiation: All of the children should note the sections' subheadings. Some children will be able to draw more important points from the text.

Back at school: In a whole-class lesson, display an enlarged version of the text 'Making electricity'. Involve the children in demonstrating how to pick out the main points and refer to their notes. Ask questions such as: *Did the pictures help you to identify key information? How easy was it to pick out the renewable sources of energy?*

Page 105 All about birds

Non-fiction objective: To write a report from notes.

Setting the homework: This homework should follow a lesson in which you have modelled how to use notes to write a report.

Differentiation: All of the children should be able to group the notes into sections based on the names of the birds. Some children will be able to use other criteria obtained from reading the information on the notes.

Back at school: Organise the children into groups of four so that they can take turns in explaining how they have organised their report.

Link to *100 Literacy Framework Lessons Y2*: NFU4, Phase 3: writing a report from notes.

Page 106 A little snivel – Core skills

Objective: To spell with increasing accuracy, drawing on knowledge of spelling patterns.

Setting the homework: Explain the both the '-el' and '-le' endings usually have the same sound – 'l'. This means that each spelling has to be learned – there are no easy rules!

Differentiation: Less confident learners should work on the first column only. Demonstrate how to say the printed part of the word and follow it immediately with an 'l' sound.

Back at school: Go over the words while children check their own sheets.

Page 107 Shopping game – Core skills

Objective: To use commas to separate items in a list.

Setting the homework: Explain how to set out the lists using the examples given at the bottom of the homework sheet. In particular, emphasise that the last item is joined by *and*, not by using a comma.

Back at school: Share some of the lists, then ask the children to write stories or descriptions that include lists, for example *What I'd like for Christmas* or *Packing for a holiday*.

Page 108 Adding '-s' – Core skills

Objective: To spell with increasing accuracy, drawing on knowledge of word structure and spelling patterns.

Setting the homework: Revise the terms 'singular' and 'plural' before explaining the sorting exercise.

Differentiation: More confident learners should be given a set of cards with words written in the singular. They should then apply the spelling rules and write the plural version of the word on the back of the card.

Back at school: Quickly go over the sorting exercise, then give the children a short list of singular words for them to pluralise by applying the four rules they investigated for homework.

Page 109 – The silence of 'lamb' – Core skills

Objective: To spell with increasing accuracy, drawing on knowledge of word structure and spelling patterns.

Setting the homework: Encourage the children to work hard on this list which contains many words that cause spelling problems and includes examples of most of the common patterns of silent letters.

Back at school: Ask the children to test each other in pairs. Revisit this list on a number of future occasions.

Poetry – Unit 1 Patterns on the page

Page 110 Hands

Poetry objective: To explore patterns created by the way words are used and the way text is laid out on the page.

Setting the homework: Read the poem aloud to the children and then with them. Ask them to look, in particular, at the verbs that end with '-ing'. Explain that they will be reading the poem at home and then writing one of their own.

Differentiation: Less confident learners who may experience difficulty in writing poems could produce list poems in which only one word (a verb) is used on each of six lines following the word *hands*.

Back at school: Ask the children to read aloud their poems, and write some of the verbs they have used on the board and discuss their spellings.

Link to *100 Literacy Framework Lessons Y2*: PU1, Phase 1: identifying patterns in poetry.

Page 111 I had a boat

Poetry objective: To explore patterns created by the way words are used and the way text is laid out on the page.

Setting the homework: Ensure that the children understand that rhyme occurs when words end with the same sound. Explain that non-rhyming poems are sometimes called *free verse*.

Differentiation: Less confident learners should try to identify which is the rhyming and which is the non-rhyming poem. More confident learners could also be asked to colour code the rhymes and try to explain the effect of the line breaks on the way the poem is read.

Back at school: Ask the children to look through a poetry anthology that contains rhyming and non-rhyming poems and to pick out several examples of each.

Link to *100 Literacy Framework Lessons Y2*: PU1, Phase 1: identifying patterns in poetry.

Page 112 Homework poem

Poetry objective: To write simple texts following a given pattern.

Setting the homework: Explain that poetry is language made into patterns. The most well-known pattern is rhyme, but repetition is also very effective and is easier to write. Ask the children to read the poem then to add more excuses to finish it.

Differentiation: Less confident learners could omit the second task.

Back at school: Share the excuses written by the children. Combine the excuses into a new whole-class poem. When several excuses have been jotted on the board, discuss which order to write them in. The class might decide, for example, to end with the funniest or most ridiculous.

Link to *100 Literacy Framework Lessons Y2*: PU1, Phase 3: adding lines to humorous poetry.

Page 113 Shapes with meaning

Poetry objective: To create a patterned poem.

Setting the homework: Children should approach this homework having already experienced collecting ideas from first-hand evidence, such as objects and natural phenomena like rain and snow. Demonstrate, as part of a whole-class lesson on writing poetry, how useful collections of ideas and words are for creating poetry.

Differentiation: All of the children should decide on what ideas and words they want to include in their poem. Some children will be able to assemble their ideas and words into a shape poem.

Back at school: Choose two confident children to talk through their thinking of how they assembled their ideas into a shape poem which should be enlarged and on display for them to refer to.

Link to *100 Literacy Framework Lessons Y2*: PU1, Phase 2: exploring patterns in shape poems.

Page 114 Months of the year – Core skills

Objective: To read high and medium frequency words independently and automatically.

Setting the homework: Explain to the children that the poem describes what the poet thinks each month of the year brings. Ask them to read the poem at home with their helpers and then practise the order of the months and how to spell them.

Differentiation: Some children might not be asked to learn all of the spellings of the months but could be limited to some of the simpler names such as *March, April, May, June* and *July*. More confident learners could be asked to write their own poems or parts of poems for the months.

Back at school: Hold an informal spelling quiz to see if the children are able to spell the names of the months. Discuss some of the similarities or common features of the spellings of some months, for example *January* and *February*; and *September, October, November* and *December*.

Page 115 Words within words (2) – Core skills

Objective: To spell with increasing accuracy, drawing on knowledge of word structure and spelling patterns.

Setting the homework: Explain the game to the children by going over the rules on the sheet and writing an example on the board, such as *blackcurrant – black, currant, lack, rant, ant, an*.

Differentiation: This will largely be by outcome, according to the number of words children find. A similar word-finding activity, 'Words within words (1)', which may be more suitable for some children, appears on page 87.

Back at school: Go over some of the words on the cards, inviting children to suggest words that they found.

Poetry – Unit 2 Really looking

Page 116 Winter morning

Poetry objective: To read and respond to poems based on closely observed experiences.

Setting the homework: Explain to the children that they will be given a poem to read and that there are some questions that they will need to answer.

Back at school: Look at the poem with the whole class and answer the questions together. Talk about other poems that the children know and ask them to answer similar questions. If some children looked at other poems for their homework, make use of these.

Page 117 Noses

Poetry objective: To read and respond to poems based on closely observed experiences.

Setting the homework: Explain that the children will be reading a poem and looking for rhyming words in it. You may wish to read the poem to the class first.

Differentiation: You may wish to ask parents and helpers of less confident learners to read the poem aloud, encouraging the children to join in where they are able.

Back at school: Read the poem with the children and ask them to identify the rhyming words. Write these on the board and ask the class to suggest further words that would rhyme with them. Talk about the different spelling patterns that can be used to create the same sounds.

Page 118 I only see middles
Poetry objective: To read with expression a poem related to own closely observed experience.
Setting the homework: Tell the children to think about the poem in relation to themselves so that they can practise reading it aloud with expression.
Differentiation: All of the children should be able to read the poem with expression. Some children should be encouraged to learn the poem so that they can perform reciting it to others.
Back at school: Extend this activity by asking the children to think of other ways in which they are affected by not being as tall as adults and to see if they can express their feelings about this in their own poems.
Link to *100 Literacy Framework Lessons Y2*: PU2, Phase 1: relating poems to own experience.

Page 119 Look, listen and feel
Poetry objective: To plan own poem based on direct experience.
Setting the homework: Explain to the children that the pictures on the homework sheet are to help them get started on the process of composing a poem and that it is the process that is important at this point. Where possible, they should look at the real thing rather than just the pictures in order to experience more.
Differentiation: All of the children should collect ideas about what they see, hear and feel about their chosen object. Some children will need more experience of collecting ideas by using the pictures on the homework sheet as a starting point.
Back at school: With the permission of a child, model the composition process from the collection of the child's ideas to a completed piece of poetry.
Link to *100 Literacy Framework Lessons Y2*: PU2, Phase 3: writing descriptive poetry.

Page 120 Cluttered desk – Core skills
Objective: To use commas to separate items in a list.
Setting the homework: Note that children will sometimes find commas used before *and*. Explain that a comma is used before *and* only if the writer wants to emphasise the last item.
Differentiation: More confident learners could be asked to make up a number of additional lists.
Back at school: Go over the homework. Remember to allow for differences of interpretation of the pictures. The main thing is that the sequence of commas and *and* should be correct.

Page 121 Long vowels – Core skills
Objective: To spell with increasing accuracy, drawing on knowledge of word structure and spelling patterns.
Setting the homework: Revise the term 'vowel'. The homework focuses on long vowels. The long sound is the name of the letter: *bay, see, pile, cone, tune*. Long vowel phonemes can be spelled in many different ways. Explain to the children that they should think of their own examples.
Differentiation: Less confident learners should be encouraged to find as many as they can. More confident learners could be asked to think of several examples and use them in sentences.
Back at school: Share all the examples. Write them on the board. This will be helpful to any less confident learners who may have left gaps.

Poetry – Unit 3 Silly stuff

Page 122 Knock, knock
Poetry objective: To read and respond to humorous texts that play with language.
Setting the homework: Explain that 'Knock, knock' jokes are like little free-verse poems because they all follow a set pattern. Encourage the children to enjoy reading these jokes and to write some of their own.
Back at school: Share the children's jokes.

Page 123 Sandwich fillings

Poetry objective: To discuss why a text is funny or surprising.

Setting the homework: Talk about different types of humour. Ask the children to read the poem and talk about why it is funny. They should all try to write a similar poem and then, if they feel able, try to write a different type of poem and compare it with the one on the homework sheet.

Back at school: Share the children's poems. Discuss the different types of humorous poems that they know and say why they are funny, building up a class list of the ways poets and authors create humour.

Link to *100 Literacy Framework Lessons Y2*: PU3, Phase 1: identifying humour in words.

Page 124 What nonsense!

Poetry objective: To write silly verse in response to prompts.

Setting the homework: This homework should follow a lesson where you have modelled composing silly poems by inventing silly words. Tell the children to invent words rather than labour trying to find words that fit.

Differentiation: All of the children should be able to invent silly words. Some will be able to adapt and modify their words to fit the rhythm of the nursery rhyme frame.

Back at school: Organise the children into groups of four so that they can take turns to share their invented words and silly poems. Make a class book of the poems for children to refer to in future.

Link to *100 Literacy Framework Lessons Y2*: PU3, Phase 3: creating humour in poetry.

Page 125 Solomon Grundy – Core skills

Objective: To read high and medium frequency words independently and automatically.

Setting the homework: Explain to the children that their homework activity should help them to remember the names of the days of the week and that they should also learn how to spell them.

Differentiation: More confident learners could be asked to write a simple rhyme with their parents/helpers which would help others to remember the sequence of days of the week.

Back at school: Conduct a simple spelling quiz to check if children are able to spell the names of the days of the week. Help them to remember how to spell *Wednesday* by teaching them to remember its mispronunciation *Wed-nes-day*.

Page 126 Alliterative sentences – Core skills

Objective: To make adventurous word and language choices appropriate to the style and purpose of the text.

Setting the homework: Explain that the children will need to write sentences beginning with the same sound. They should use the characters in the pictures as a starting point. You might like to work through one example together, such as *Winnie the wicked witch watches wiggly worms*.

Differentiation: This will largely be by outcome, with more confident learners producing longer and more adventurous sentences.

Back at school: Ask the children to share examples of their alliterative sentences with the rest of the class.

Page 127 Chefs and chiefs – Core skills

Objective: To spell with increasing accuracy, drawing on knowledge of word structure and spelling patterns.

Setting the homework: Go over the explanation, and emphasise the importance of learning the exceptions.

Back at school: Monitor the application of this spelling rule. The children could find other exceptions through their reading.

NARRATIVE

Name	Date

Lost on the beach

■ Read this story with your helper.

"Don't go into the deep water and stay where we can see you!"

I could hear my mother's words as I ran towards the sea across the crowded beach. I dashed past toddlers digging in the sand; skipped around parents and children who were building sandcastles; and walked carefully past sunbathers in case I kicked sand onto them.

The soft white sand, which was so pleasant to walk on, soon became stony as I neared the sea. The pebbles and rocks hurt my feet and I picked my way across the beach, all the time saying, "Ow, ow, ouch!"

After the stones, the sand was wet and covered with slippery seaweed. I tried to avoid walking on it, but once I almost slipped and fell over.

Finally, I reached the water's edge. The tide was coming in and children waited for the waves to come crashing towards them before running, screaming and laughing to try to avoid getting soaked. I joined in and managed to run away three times before an extra large wave came in too fast for me and washed over me as I stumbled. The water was cold and my teeth chattered, but I didn't mind. I was enjoying myself.

After about half an hour, I remembered my parents and decided I had better go back and tell them I was all right. They worried if they didn't know where I was. I turned my back on the sea and began to walk inland. The seaweed seemed to have almost disappeared but the stony part of the beach was as big as before and I felt my feet getting sore.

I stopped to rest and looked up the beach to where I thought my parents would be, but I could not see them at all. They had a blue and yellow windbreak and a matching umbrella to shade them from the sun. As I looked around, I could see dozens of umbrellas that were just like ours. I began to panic. I must have moved along the beach when I was playing, and now I did not recognise any of the people I could see. Everyone on the beach seemed so happy, but I was feeling very unhappy indeed.

Illustrations © Pete Smith/Beehive Illustration.

Dear helper
Objective: To understand time and sequence in stories.
Task: Read the story with your child. Talk to them about the sequence of events in the story and the order they occur in. Discuss what might happen next. Ask questions, such as: *Do you think that the character will find their parents? How do you think they might do this?*

Name   Date

It was only yesterday

■ Read the story below with your helper and then retell
it, keeping it in the past tense.

Emma was feeling much happier today. Yesterday had been a big day
for her. For the very first time she had managed to talk in front of the whole class.
Emma had not been at the school very long. She had just moved from Scotland and
left all her friends behind. Hardest of all was that now she lived with her mum and did
not see her dad often, or her grandparents. She particularly missed her grandad. He
sometimes seemed the only one who understood how she felt.

Emma had found it very hard to make friends with the children at her new school.
They laughed at her funny accent, and at playtimes she usually walked round the
playground on her own. She was even shyer in class and hardly ever said anything.

This term all the children had to take turns to bring in a special object to talk about
to the class. Emma had made excuses and tried to avoid taking her turn, but finally
the time came when Emma's teacher told her it was her turn. Emma had pleaded
that she didn't have anything special to show, not like some of the other children. Her
teacher said it did not need to be anything amazing, but something special to her. She
told Emma about a special necklace that her grandmother had given her. Every time
she looked at it, it reminded her of her grandmother. That gave Emma an idea.

The next day Emma came to school clutching a small object wrapped in paper.
When the teacher said, "Now, it's Emma's turn," Emma stood up timidly and went
to fetch the object from her drawer. Slowly she unwrapped the object and the class
gazed in anticipation. As Emma stared at the small object she seemed to gain
confidence and began to speak.

"This was my grandad's tobacco tin," she began to explain. She opened the
lid and sniffed it and, as she carefully passed it around for the class to smell, she
explained how that smell was special to her. Emma described her grandad, how
he always had a funny tobacco smell, but how he talked to her and knew just how
she felt. She talked about the things they did together, such as helping him at his
allotment. Suddenly this shy girl changed to the whole class. Everyone felt as if
they knew her grandfather when she had finished, and her teacher just looked in
amazement. The class all clapped and for the first time Emma felt she belonged.

At playtime lots of children crowded round her and wanted to talk to her and she
began to make friends. That night she wrote a letter to her grandad and told him all
about it. He didn't seem so far away now.

Illustrations © Pete Smith/Beehive Illustration.

Dear helper
Objective: To be able to retell a story in the past tense.
Task: This activity will help your child to recall a story and tell it in the past tense. Read the story with them
and talk about the main events. Now help them to retell the story, ensuring they keep it in the past tense.

NARRATIVE

Name   Date

Helping a friend

◼ Read the short story 'Helping a friend'.

Robert and David were playing tag with some friends in the playground. Robert loved running and dodging but, as so often happens to Robert, he fell over and bumped his knees, leaving him crying in a heap. David ran over to him to help.

"Hey Rob," he called, "don't cry, you'll be ok."

Just as David was bending down to help him up, the girl who was tag tapped him on the shoulder shouting, "You're it! You're it! I've tagged you!"

David did not think he should explain to her that it was unfair to tag while in the middle of helping someone, so he just said, "Ok, but you'll have to wait for me until Rob feels better."

Robert's knees were quite red and grazed so David cupped his warm hands around them.

"Thanks mate," said Robert.

◼ Read the questions and discuss the answers with your helper.

1. What did David do when Robert fell over? What does this tell you about David?
2. What did David say to Robert when he fell over? What does this tell you about David?
3. What did David think when the girl tagged him? What does this tell you about David?
4. Why did David reply to the girl in the way he did?
5. What did David do when he saw that Robert's knees were red and grazed? What does this tell you about David?
6. What did Robert say to David at the end of the story? Why is this important in telling you a lot more about David?

Illustrations © Pete Smith/Beehive Illustration.

Dear helper
Objective: To find out about character from what is done, said, felt and thought.
Task: Read the short story with your child. Tell your child that you are going to use the questions to show how a character's actions, words, thoughts and feelings can reveal the character's personality.

Name	Date

The school trip

◢ Read the story and answer the questions.

Alex was excited. Today was the day they were
going on the school trip to the seaside. He had
been a few times before, but his mum did not
have a car, so they had to go on a coach and it was much too
expensive to go often. He was soon dressed, had eaten his
breakfast and was nagging Mum to take him to school.

"Not yet, Alex. It's not time. Now just make sure you have got
everything – packed lunch, drink, spending money and a pair of
shorts and hat in case it is hot."

Alex made sure for the hundredth time that it was all there
in his bag and, at last, it was time to go. As soon as he got to
school, he saw the coach waiting. Some of the others were
already waiting in the playground and Mrs Gray, his teacher,
was checking she had everything, including the sick bucket!

Finally, they were on their way! Alex sat next to Simon, his
best friend, and everything was going according to plan. He had
no idea how badly it was all going to turn out.

1. Why was it special for Alex to go to the seaside?

_____

2. What did Alex have to remember to take with him?

_____

3. Who did Alex sit next to on the coach?

_____

Illustrations © Pete Smith/Beehive Illustration.

Dear helper
Objective: To be able to answer questions on a story.
Task: Read the story with your child and then read the questions together. Help your child to write the
answers, remembering to write in full sentences.

NARRATIVE

Name

Date

The school trip – how does it end?

■ Read the story with your helper.

Alex was excited. Today was the day they were going on the school trip to the seaside. He had been a few times before, but his mum did not have a car, so they had to go on a coach and it was much too expensive to go often. He was soon dressed, had eaten his breakfast and was nagging Mum to take him to school.

"Not yet, Alex. It's not time. Now just make sure you have got everything – packed lunch, drink, spending money and a pair of shorts and hat in case it is hot."

Alex made sure for the hundredth time that it was all there in his bag and, at last, it was time to go. As soon as he got to school, he saw the coach waiting. Some of the others were already waiting in the playground and Mrs Gray, his teacher, was checking she had everything, including the sick bucket!

Finally, they were on their way! Alex sat next to Simon, his best friend, and everything was going according to plan. He had no idea how badly it was all going to turn out.

■ Now write what happens next. You can use the back of this sheet. Think about what could have gone wrong and why.

Illustrations © Pete Smith/Beehive Illustration.

Dear helper
Objective: To be able to write an ending to a story.
Task: Talk with your child about a possible ending and encourage them to use their imagination. Ask: *Did Alex get lost? Did someone get hurt? How did Alex feel and what did he do?*

Name	Date

Missing mouse

■ Read the story together and then talk about how you think it might end. Write down your ending on a separate sheet of paper.

"Why can't they leave the poor thing alone?" muttered Amy to herself.

She held the tiny mouse in her hands, taking care to keep it hidden under her coat. She was sure that it was trembling. It must have been frightened of her, but Amy would never hurt it.

All around her people were yelling and shouting and calling things like: "Over there! I think I saw it." The mouse had appeared in the classroom just as the children were getting ready to go out to play. Everyone had rushed in from the cloakroom when they heard Mrs Brady screaming. They had found their teacher standing on a chair looking around herself nervously.

The caretaker had been fetched and so had Miss Fleming and Miss Urmston. The adults and most of the children rushed around the room looking for the mouse. Only Amy knew where it was. She had seen it under her desk and had picked it up quickly before anyone had a chance to see. Now she wanted to protect it from all the people who wanted to catch it.

Illustrations © Pete Smith/Beehive Illustration.

Dear helper
Objective: To predict story endings.
Task: Read the story together and talk about any words that your child finds difficult. Discuss possible endings for the story before your child begins writing.

NARRATIVE

Name   Date

What happened and when?

◀ Look at the story frame below and use it to plan a story.

(Beginning)

(Something happens)

(Events to sort it out)

(Ending)

Illustrations © Pete Smith/Beehive Illustration.

Dear helper
Objective: To plan the sequence of events in a story.
Task: Help your child to think of ideas for each section. Discuss the importance of trying out ideas and changing them if we think of better ones. Remind your child that writers rewrite and check spellings.

PHOTOCOPIABLE 📖SCHOLASTIC
www.scholastic.co.uk

At the seaside

deckchair	waves	sandcastle	seaweed
windbreak	umbrella	ice cream	spade
bucket	beach		

What to do

1. Cut out the picture and word cards.
2. Spread the cards out – the picture cards face up and the word cards face down.
3. Turn over a word card. Read it and then match it to the correct picture card.

Dear helper
Objective: To learn new words linked to a particular topic: the seaside.
Task: Read the words together and, if necessary, help your child to match the words to the pictures. Then turn all the cards face down and take it in turns to turn two cards over to find matching word and picture pairs. If your child feels confident enough to do so, they can write down the words on paper.

Illustrations © Pete Smith/Beehive Illustration.

CORE SKILLS

Name

Date

What's black and white and read all over?

"What is black and white and read all over?" asked Shamin.

Jenny thought for a moment and then replied, "I don't know. What is black and white and red all over?"

"A newspaper!" said Shamin with a smile.

Jenny looked puzzled. "But newspapers aren't red," she grumbled.

Shamin laughed. "They're not red the colour, but they are read because people read them."

Jenny groaned. She decided she would get her own back after Shamin's joke. "Right Shamin, if you're so clever let's see if you can do this: Wednesday is a very hard word. Can you spell it?"

"Easy," laughed Shamin, "w-e-d-n…"

Before she could say any more, Jenny interrupted. "No, you've got it wrong!"

"Of course I haven't. It's w-e-d…"

Jenny interrupted again. "No it isn't. Fancy you not even being able to spell a simple word like it."

"But you asked me to spell Wednesday," complained Shamin.

"No I didn't. What I said was, 'Wednesday is a very hard word. Can you spell it?' It is spelled i-t."

Now it was Shamin's turn to groan.

■ Underline the words that the girls spoke.

■ Now take the part of one of the girls and ask your helper to be the other one. Have the conversation that Jenny and Shamin had, but remember only to say the words that they actually spoke.

Illustrations © Pete Smith/Beehive Illustration.

Dear helper

Objective: To identify speech marks in reading and understand their purpose.

Task: Read the dialogue with your child and look at the speech marks. Help your child to identify the words that are spoken, then hold the conversation together.

Name	Date

In the past

■ Rewrite the sentences in the past tense.
The first one has been done for you.

1. Mrs Jones is going to the market.

   Mrs Jones went to the market.

2. Edward helps a neighbour.

   _____

3. The girl takes a plant to her mother.

   _____

4. Jonathan plays dominoes.

   _____

5. Salma makes a cake.

   _____

6. The dog jumps over the fence.

   _____

Illustrations © Pete Smith/Beehive Illustration.

Dear helper
Objective: To be able to write in the past tense.
Task: Help your child to read the sentences and then put them in the past tense (remind your child that this means that the event happened before). If they are having difficulty, suggest they say their new sentences aloud, saying *Yesterday...* at the beginning of each one.

Name   Date

Words we use a lot

■ Read the words below and then look at the piece of writing you've been given by your teacher.

■ Underline the words in the piece of writing that can be found in the suitcase. For example:

Don't go into the deep water, and stay where we can see you!

after   again   all   and   away

but   came   can   come   could

don't   for   from   go   had

just   like   me   my   not

now   once   over   people   see

so   them   they   time   to

too   very   was   were   where

who   with   would   yellow   you

Illustrations © Pete Smith/Beehive Illustration.

Dear helper
Objective: To be able to read words that occur frequently.
Task: Help your child to read the words above and the piece of writing that accompanies this homework. Ask your child to find the words in the text and underline them. Talk about the spellings of the words. If your child feels sufficiently confident, they could look at some words, one by one, cover them and then write them.

Name	Date

Sack and the Jeanstalk

◾ Read this funny extract from the story of 'Sack and the Jeanstalk'.

◾ Underline all the words that are wrong. Then rewrite the correct story of 'Jack and the Beanstalk' next to the pictures.

Once upon a line there was a boy called Jack.
He lived with his mother in a little mouse.
Jack's mother was a poor window.
Now Jack was a very lazy toy.

One day all they had left was the cow.
So Jack took the sow to market to sell her.

On the way he met a man.
"Would you swap your cow for these magic jeans?"
"Oh yes," said Jack.

Dee Reid

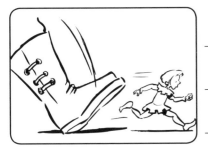

Dear helper

Objective: To write sentences to fit a known story.

Task: Read the alternative version of 'Jack and the Beanstalk' and ask your child to underline all the wrong words. Talk about the original story and ask your child to look carefully at the pictures showing the beginning, middle and end of the story. Help them to write sentences to fit each picture.

NARRATIVE

Name   Date

Troll's noisy problem

- Read the story with your helper.
- Discuss how the story is different from the traditional tale.

Once upon a time there were three Billy Goats Gruff and a Troll. The three Billy Goats Gruff lived in a field on one side of a river with a rickety wooden bridge; under the bridge lived the Troll.

Trip-trap over the bridge went little Billy Goat Gruff. He was only half way across when up popped the Troll.

"I say, would you mind not clattering your hoofs on the bridge. It makes such a din down here and the bridge is none too strong you know," said the Troll.

"I can do what I like because my brother is coming across after me and he is much bigger than I am and if he knows you have been trying to tell me what to do he'll sort you out. So there!" said little Billy Goat Gruff and off he went with his nose in the air.

"Oh dear," said the Troll sadly and went back under the bridge.

Trip-trap over the bridge went middle-sized Billy Goat Gruff. He was only half way across when up popped the Troll.

"I say, would you mind not clattering your hoofs on the bridge. It makes such a din down here and the bridge is none too strong you know," said the Troll.

"I can do what I like because my brother is coming across after me and he is much bigger than I am and if he knows you have been trying to tell me what to do he'll sort you out. So there!" said middle-sized Billy Goat Gruff and off he went with his nose in the air to join his brother on the other side.

"Oh dear," said the Troll sadly and again he went back under the bridge.

TRIP-TRAP over the bridge went great-big Billy Goat Gruff. He was only half way across when up popped the Troll. He was about to ask great-big Billy Goat Gruff to not make so much noise when the other two Billy Goats Gruff clattered across the bridge to meet their brother. They told their brother what the Troll had said to them.

"Right!" said great-big Billy Goat Gruff, "We'll show him!" and they began trip-trapping up and down the bridge so loudly the Troll had to put his hands to his ears. Just when he thought he couldn't stand any more there was a loud crack and the bridge gave way. The three Billy Goats Gruff were swept away down the river.

"Well, I did try and tell them that the bridge wouldn't stand all that trip-trapping!" said the Troll.

Dear helper
Objective: To identify and talk about how this story differs from the traditional tale.
Task: Watch together the traditional version of the story on http://ngfl.northumberland.gov.uk/english/goats/billygoatsgruff.html, read the traditional story together, or tell the story in your own words. Then read together 'Troll's noisy problem' and discuss with your child how, from the Troll's point of view, the story is very different. Why is it that the Troll and the three Billy Goats Gruff seem so different in this version?

Name	Date

Say and do

◼ Identify the good characters and the villains by what they say and do.

Dear helper

Objective: To identify the good characters and the villains by what they say and do.

Task: Look at the pictures with your child. Talk about how the actions of the characters and what they say can tell us a lot about characters. Ask your child what the pictures and words tell us about each character and help them to decide if the character is good or a villain. Read the traditional story together, tell the stories in your own words or find online versions at websites such as www.bbc.co.uk/cbeebies/stories.

NARRATIVE

Name   Date

From good to bad

◢ Imagine if Little Red Riding Hood and Cinderella changed from being kind, helpful and polite characters into characters who are not. Write what they might say in the empty speech bubbles.

I'll cheer grandma up with some cakes.

Grandma, can I help? You look tired.

I will clean the kitchen.

Please can I go to the ball?

Illustrations © Pete Smith/Beehive Illustration.

Dear helper
Objective: To rewrite dialogue in order to change the traditional roles of characters.
Task: Discuss with your child why what is being said in the speech bubbles on the left-hand side of the page is helpful in creating a picture of Red Riding Hood and Cinderella. Talk about using what they say to show a different side of Red Riding Hood and Cinderella. Support your child in writing the dialogue.

PHOTOCOPIABLE ▲SCHOLASTIC
www.scholastic.co.uk

NARRATIVE

Name   Date

Two different people?

◗ Read about Jordan. Then change the words that are in bold so that, instead of being unpleasant, Jordan is a pleasant person. Write about the pleasant Jordan in the box.

Mean Jordan

Jordan was a very **mean** boy. He **never** gave his friends **any** sweets and he **never** shared his crisps. He had **few** friends and **no one** liked him very much. The only time he was **happy** was when another child fell over or got into trouble with a teacher.

Pleasant Jordan

◗ Write down in pairs the bold words from 'Mean Jordan' and the opposite words (antonyms) which you used in 'Pleasant Jordan'. Use a separate sheet of paper.

Illustrations © Pete Smith/Beehive Illustration.

Dear helper
Objective: To understand the use of opposites and to discuss differences of meaning.
Task: Read the text together and talk about the words in bold. These words will alter the text's meaning if they are changed. Go on to write pairs of opposites made up of the bold words from the original text and the changed words from the new version. At school, your child will have heard the term *antonyms* for opposites, so you can use this term with them.

NARRATIVE

Name   Date

What's in a picture?

◼ Look at the pictures. What do they tell you about Cinderella?

Illustrations © Pete Smith/Beehive Illustration.

Dear helper
Objective: To determine Cinderella's character from the images.
Task: Watch together the story of Cinderella at www.bbc.co.uk/cbeebies/stories (find Cinderella in the A to Z menu), read the traditional story together, or tell the story in your own words. Ask your child what each image means to Cinderella and discuss how they might affect Cinderella's character.

PHOTOCOPIABLE 📖SCHOLASTIC

www.scholastic.co.uk

Name | Date

Birthday ball

- Read the beginning of the story 'Birthday ball'.
- Continue to write the story in your own words so that Cinderella meets the Prince at his birthday ball.
- Use the words in the box to help you.

Once upon a time when a lonely Prince was riding in his forest he had an idea. "I know. I will hold a ball to celebrate my birthday." He thought this was a really good idea because he would get to meet lots of people and maybe, just maybe, the girl he would want to marry. When he was back at the palace he organised for invitations to be sent to everyone in his principality. Meanwhile at Cinderella's house

_____

_____

_____

_____

_____

_____

_____

_____

_____

_____

| when | then | because | so | meanwhile | soon |
| just as | next | eventually | however | but |

Dear helper
Objective: To use connectives to write a short story.
Task: Watch the story with your child on www.bbc.co.uk/cbeebies/stories (select Cinderella from the A to Z menu), read the traditional story together, or tell the story in your own words. Support your child in composing the rest of the story explaining how the connecting words help to link events together.

Name   Date

Jill and Jack

■ Read the story.

It was a long way up the steep hill. The children, whose names were Jill and Jack, took turns to carry the bucket. In the distance, they could see the well.

"Can't we stop for a rest?" asked Jack after a few minutes.

"No," replied Jill. "We have to get the bucket of water to Mum quickly, if we want any dinner."

The children carried on climbing the hill. Below them they could see the town of Bilton, and they spotted their own house with smoke coming from the chimney.

Finally, they reached the top of the hill and lowered the bucket deep into the well. It took ages before they heard the bucket splash into the water. They pulled it up again and poured the water into their own bucket. As Jack tried to pick up the full bucket, he stumbled and fell. The water spilled as Jill tried to stop Jack from tumbling down the hill. She slipped and rolled down the hill after her brother.

"Ouch, that hurt!" grumbled Jack as he stood up at the bottom of the hill.

"Thank goodness we're both all right," said Jill. "Now we'd better climb all the way back to the top of the hill again!"

Illustrations © Pete Smith/Beehive Illustration.

■ Put a line under all the capital letters.

  ☐ Draw a ring ◯ around those which have capitals because they begin sentences or speech.

  ☐ Draw a box ☐ around those which have capitals because they are special names.

Dear helper
Objective: To revise knowledge about the use of capital letters.
Task: Read the story with your child and identify the words that begin with capital letters. Talk about the reason for the capital letters. Do they signify a special name, the beginning of a sentence or paragraph, or the beginning of speech?

Name	Date

Talking to the giant

- Read carefully what the giant and Jack are saying.
- Put the missing full stops, question marks and exclamation marks into the speech bubbles.

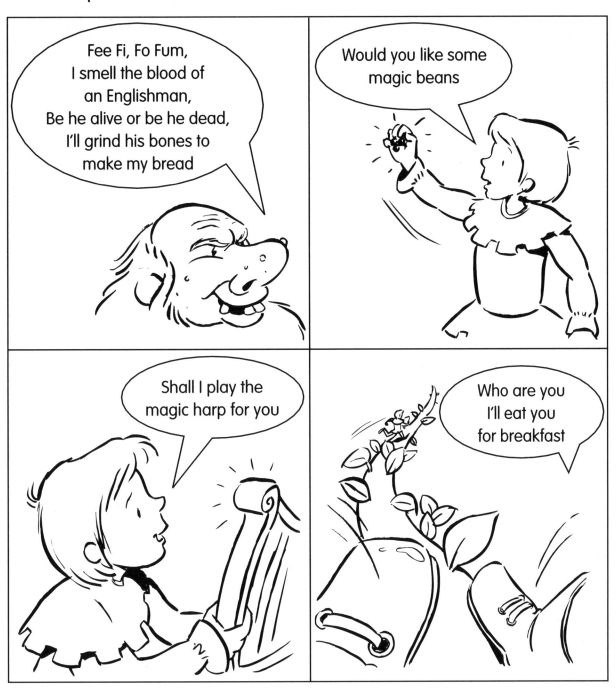

Illustrations © Pete Smith/Beehive Illustration.

Dear helper

Objective: To be able to use question marks and exclamation marks correctly.

Task: Ask your child to look carefully at the pictures and read the words in the speech bubbles with expression. Talk about the correct punctuation and help them to write it in. You can also help them to write the speech out using speech marks and correct punctuation on the back of the sheet.

Name   Date

Opposites

■ Look at the two lists of words. Draw lines to join the words that have opposite meanings. One has been done for you.

good	low
happy	below
kind	light
high	unkind
like	stay
dark	upstairs
above	unhappy
go	silly
downstairs	dislike
sensible	bad

■ Now make your own jumbled lists of opposites and join the pairs with lines.

Illustrations © Pete Smith/Beehive Illustration.

Dear helper
Objective: To understand the use of opposites and to discuss differences of meaning.
Task: Look at the words in each list together and then work out the opposites for each one. Your child may have heard the word *antonym* at school and may use this word for *opposite*. Talk about opposites and try saying some simple words (that have opposites) and asking your child to tell you some possible opposites.

Name   Date

Find the opposite

■ Look at the list of words and write **at least one** word for each that has an opposite meaning. The first one has been started for you.

little	big, large
hard	
empty	
in	
up	
some	
hot	
raw	
obey	
near	
undo	
agree	
before	
with	
appear	
first	

Illustrations © Pete Smith/Beehive Illustration.

Dear helper

Objective: To understand the use of opposites and to discuss differences of meaning.

Task: Look at the words in the left-hand column with your child and read them aloud. Ask your child to suggest opposites for each one. Your child may have heard the word *antonym* at school and may use this word for *opposite*. There may be more than one opposite for some words (for example, the opposite of *hard* could be *soft* or *easy*). Help your child to write the opposites in the boxes next to the words and discuss spellings.

NARRATIVE

Name _____ Date _____

My opinion

- Choose a book you have read recently or one you are reading now.
- Use the questions to help you express your opinion about the story.

Book title: _____

Author: _____

What would you tell a friend about the book?

_____

_____

Was there a character that you particularly liked and why?

_____

_____

Did the pictures add to your understanding of the story?

_____

_____

How did the setting add to the story?

_____

_____

Did you find the story too long, too short or just right and why?

_____

_____

Did you enjoy reading it and why?

_____

_____

Did this book make you want to read other books by this author?

_____

_____

Dear helper
Objective: To be able to express opinions and explain them.
Task: Use the questions to support a discussion with your child about a story. Help your child to express and expand ideas and opinions.

Name _____ Date _____

About the author

◼ Choose one of your favourite authors.

◼ Use the internet to find out about your author.

◼ Use the sheet below to record the information you find out.

Author _____

Interesting facts

Where did the author live as a child? _____

Where does the author live now? _____

When did the author start to write? _____

Other things that interest you about the author:

_____

_____

_____

The author's books

What type of stories has your author written? Are they:

adventure stories ☐   funny stories ☐

ghost stories ☐   historical stories ☐

other kinds of stories ☐   poems ☐

Which ones have you read?

_____

_____

_____

Which ones would you like to read and why?

_____

_____

_____

Dear helper
Objective: To find out interesting information about an author.
Task: Encourage your child to find out about an author whose books may have been read at school. Together, use the internet to search for information about the author by typing the author's name into a search engine. Use the sheet to guide you and your child through the information, discussing the interesting facts you find out.

Name   Date

Pen portrait

◼ Choose a book you have read recently or one you are reading now.

◼ Choose your favourite character and draw the character's picture in the portrait frame.

What your character says.

What your character does.

What your character thinks.

What others think and say about your character.

◼ Write some words and phrases to describe your character.

_____

_____

Dear helper
Objective: To describe a character from a story.
Task: Help your child to choose a character from a familiar book. Ask them to draw the character in the portrait frame. Discuss with your child what the character says, does and thinks and write their ideas in the appropriate speech bubble. Then discuss what other characters think about the character and fill in the final speech bubble. Finally, use the information to make a list of words and phrases that describe the character.

PHOTOCOPIABLE ◼**SCHOLASTIC**
www.scholastic.co.uk

Name   Date

Character sketches

✂

Daisy is a happy, smiling, fair-haired girl. She likes to wear jeans and a T-shirt and loves to play football.	
Rashid has dark hair that is always smartly combed. He dresses smartly and enjoys playing tennis.	
Adam rarely combs his hair and he seems to love getting as dirty as possible whenever he goes out to play. His clothes are always full of holes.	
Mrs Owen wears a thick coat whenever she goes out, even when it is hot and sunny. She always seems to be in a hurry and usually looks rather serious.	
Natalie is always being cross with people. She has long, dark hair which she wears in a pony tail.	
Mr Ferguson is always looking at his watch and looking worried. He has a moustache and wears smart suits and ties.	

◼ Cut out the descriptions and the pictures. Read the descriptions of the characters and match them to the pictures. When you have done this, try writing a character sketch of someone you know and drawing a picture to go with it.

Illustrations © Pete Smith/Beehive Illustration.

Dear helper
Objective: To identify and describe characters.
Task: Read each of the descriptions with your child and then help them to decide which of the pictures fits each description. Look, in particular, at the adjectives and see if they are reflected in the pictures. Help your child to write a character sketch for someone else and to draw a matching picture.

Name	Date

In character

■ Choose to be either character A or B and, with your helper, read the dialogue in the speech bubbles.

Character A

Where did you find that?

I thought friends shared everything, even secret places.

Now I know you have a secret place you had better keep it as your secret.

I haven't seen you near my house except when we have been playing together.

Character B

I am not telling you, it was in a secret place.

Not this secret place!

I will, even though it's near your house.

I don't just play with you. Anyway you cannot see me when I am behind your garage.

Dear helper
Objective: To find out about characters through what is said.
Task: The dialogue above is spoken by two characters in a story – A and B. What does their conversation tell you about what sort of people they are? Take turns to be the characters and model reading with expression.

Name   Date

Invent a character

▪ Use this sheet to help you create a character.

▪ Use the plan to think of a story about your character.

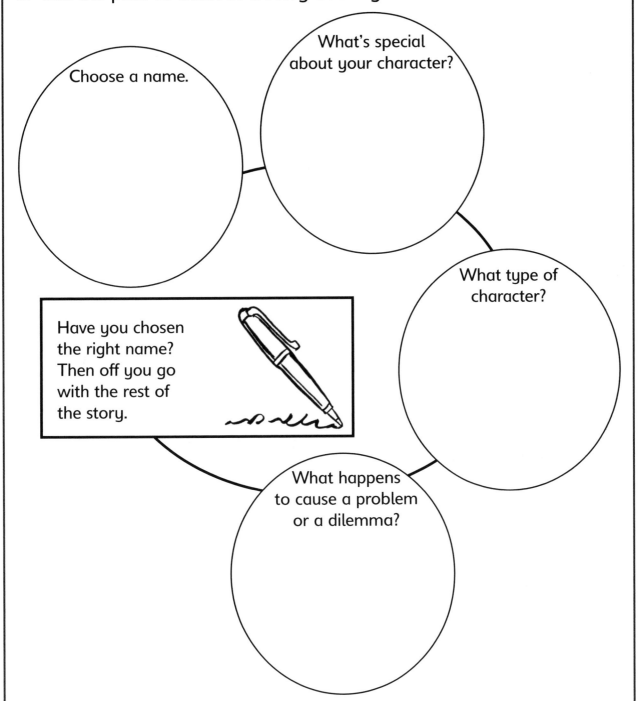

Choose a name.

What's special about your character?

What type of character?

Have you chosen the right name? Then off you go with the rest of the story.

What happens to cause a problem or a dilemma?

Illustrations © Pete Smith/Beehive Illustration.

Dear helper

Objective: To create a character upon which to base a story.

Task: Tell your child that together you are going to write a story about your child's invented character. Use the planner to help your child to decide upon a character and then to create a story around that character. Support your child by discussing the words you can use to describe the character and how that character would behave when faced with the problem/dilemma your child has decided on.

Name   Date

Stop throwing paint!

■ Choose one of the words in the box to complete each of the sentences. There may be more than one word that fits, but you should choose the one that you think fits best to write in the space.

answered	shouted	asked	replied	whispered	grumbled	yelled

"Stop throwing paint at each other!" _____ the teacher.

"Have you got any red paint left?" _____ Lisa.

"No," _____ Ryan.

"There's never any red when I need it," _____ Lisa.

"Why don't you pinch some from David's table while he's not looking?" _____ Ryan.

"Because Miss Cole will be cross if she finds out," _____ Lisa.

Suddenly a voice boomed from behind the children. "Yes, Lisa, you're quite right. Miss Cole will be very cross if she catches you taking other people's paint!" _____ Miss Cole in the angry voice which she hardly ever used.

Illustrations © Pete Smith/Beehive Illustration.

Dear helper
Objective: To choose words that are appropriate to the text to fill the spaces.
Task: Read the dialogue with your child and look at the spaces. Help your child to identify the words that could be used to fill in the spaces. Encourage your child to think about what each person said and to take this into account when choosing the appropriate verb.

PHOTOCOPIABLE ■■SCHOLASTIC

www.scholastic.co.uk

Name   Date

Who said that?

▪ Look at the pictures and then look at the words that the people said. Complete the sentences by writing the verb in the past tense and the name of the person in the spaces provided. (The past tense of **say** is **said** and the past tense of **shout** is **shouted**.)

Miss Hardcastle   **Thomas**   **Sarah Shaw**

Mrs Morgan   **Mr Davies**   **Ranjit**

"Now just wait there until I tell you it's safe to cross,"

_____ . (say)

"Oh thank you. It's just what I wanted,"

_____ . (cry)

"This is delicious. I've never tasted anything like it,"

_____ . (mumble)

"Now look, you are supposed to fetch the stick when I throw it!"

_____ . (grumble)

"It's mine I tell you. You can't wear it!"

_____ . (shout)

Please can I have one? I promise I won't want anything else,"

_____ . (plead)

Dear helper
Objective: To use verb tenses with increasing accuracy in writing.
Task: Look at the pictures with your child and then read the speeches together. Help your child to complete the sentences by adding the correct verb form and the name of the person whom they think made each speech.

Name   Date

Matching past and present

◼ Look carefully at the verbs (action words).
Match the present verbs to the past verbs.
One has been done for you.

Present	Past
buy	slept
make	bought
teach	swam
sleep	went
feel	came
swim	taught
grow	felt
bring	dug
go	got
come	made
get	took
see	wanted
run	saw
want	ran
take	brought
dig	grew

Illustrations © Pete Smith/Beehive Illustration.

Dear helper
Objective: To be able to match verbs in the present and past tense.
Task: Read the list of past and present verbs with your child and help them to match the words by drawing lines to the corresponding verbs. If your child is having difficulty, try putting the words into sentences, for example: *Today I run to school, Yesterday I ran to school.*

Name	Date

What happens next?

📕 Read and predict what might happen next in the stories below.

Phoebe had fed her two chickens, Henny and Penny, said goodnight to them and closed the chickens' shed door. From the bushes the fox watched her every move.

Who would have thought a cat and a mouse could be friends. They purred and squeaked through an evening of happy regaling of their adventures, together oblivious to owl the silently perched on the branch over their heads.

Carrie's senses were on alert and when no-one else heard the latch on the gate open, she did.

Jack hoped so much that dad would get home in time for his birthday. Morning had come after a sleepless night but dad wasn't at the breakfast table as Jack had dreamt. Then he heard a key turn in the door.

Illustrations © Pete Smith/Beehive Illustration.

Dear helper
Objective: To read cliffhangers and predict what might follow.
Task: Read and look at the pictures with your child and talk about the anticipation and anxiety that they convey. Talk about what is happening and ask your child to predict what might happen next.

NARRATIVE

Name   Date

What will Francis do?

- Read the beginning of a story about a boy called Francis.
- Discuss with your helper what sort of character Francis is and what he might do in the circumstances.

Francis was in an awful mess and he didn't know to do. He kept asking himself how a boy with his intelligence could have got into a situation so as to lose Charlie, his beautiful Collie dog at the park. Everyone knew Francis was a thoughtful, kind boy who loved his Collie dog. Even his brother Freddy had said, "Charlie couldn't be in better care than with Francis, he'll look after him."

His mother, who although a little anxious, had agreed with Freddy and said, "Francis is such a responsible boy, I know I should trust him."

Francis did not want to think about all his pleas that had led to his mum agreeing with Freddy to let him take Charlie to the park. Now his worst fears were happening.

"Think, think," he said to himself, as he scrambled in and out of the nearby bushes: was this really going to help find Charlie?

Illustrations © Pete Smith/Beehive Illustration.

Dear helper
Objective: To predict and discuss what the character might do.
Task: Read the beginning of the story together and discuss what sort of character Francis is so that your child can make predictions about what Francis might do.

Name	Date

Beginnings and endings

📖 Cut out the mixed up beginnings and endings of stories.

📖 With your helper discuss which would make good beginnings and endings.

If no one ever grew up…	There never was such a clever person as Clarissa Cleverclogs.
"Well, I never, who would have thought it!"	In the garden the flowers are always in bloom.
Come and play again another day.	The treasure remained unfound.
My dad went to a wedding one day.	So you see there was room for everyone.
She could do anything she wanted.	It was a long journey to Grandfather's.
It was as if it never happened.	The children were so astounded they forgot to say thank you.
Only magic flowers open at night.	They never went back.

📖 Draw a Venn diagram like the one below on a large sheet of paper and use it to sort the beginnings and endings.

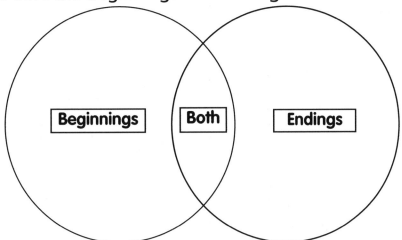

Beginnings   Both   Endings

Dear helper
Objective: To discuss and sort beginnings and endings of stories.
Task: Help your child to cut out the phrases and create a large Venn diagram as above. Discuss which of the phrases would make good beginnings and endings and arrange them into the Venn diagram. Talk about those which could be either and place them in the overlapping section of the diagram.

NARRATIVE

Name   Date

Family holiday

■ Read the story 'Family holiday' and highlight the best words to link the events in the story.

David and daddy got off the train **as soon as / after / when** it came to a stop at the station. As the train was 30 minutes late they had to rush for a taxi **in order to / so as to / to** meet mummy on time. They had to meet mummy at 3 o'clock and it was already quarter to. It was important for them to be on time **because / so** they had to catch another train which went from another station.

They got into a taxi and daddy told the taxi driver **where / that** they needed to go, telling the driver that they must be there before 3 o'clock. The taxi driver drove very fast so they would get to mummy on time. The taxi drew up outside the park gates at 5 minutes to 3 o'clock **where / then / there** they saw mummy waiting anxiously for them. **When / Because / As** she saw them in the taxi she dashed over to them and jumped into the back seat giving David and daddy a big hug each.

Daddy then told the taxi driver to drive to the next railway station where they arrived **just in time / so as** to catch the train **that would / to** take them to the seaside for their annual holiday. They were all so happy knowing what fun they **would be able / were going / were** to share together at the seaside during the next two weeks.

Illustrations © Pete Smith/Beehive Illustration.

Dear helper
Objective: To understand how linking words and phrases improve a story.
Task: Read 'Family holiday' with your child, giving support in choosing the best word or phrase that links and enhances the meaning of the narrative.

Name	Date

Connect the pictures

🔲 Use the words in the box to link the pictures and make up the story.

1.

2.

3.

Illustrations © Pete Smith/Beehive Illustration.

meanwhile	in that case	at the other side of the forest	looking in
because	however	consequently	when
inside	otherwise	so	then

Dear helper

Objective: To choose and use appropriate connective words and phrases to make a complete story.

Task: The pictures tell a different story of the traditional tale 'Little Red Riding Hood'. Together with your child, make up and tell the story choosing and using some of the connective words and phrases to help link the events in the pictures together. Then, support your child in writing the story on a separate sheet of paper using the connectives appropriately and choosing some more of your own.

Name   Date

NARRATIVE

Aladdin's adventure

◼ Read the story plot.

◼ Cut out the pictures to make nine story cards.

◼ Use the picture cards to create the story of how Aladdin rescues the Princess.

Aladdin has to rescue the beautiful princess Sabrina, held captive by the evil magician in his granite palace. There are obstacles to overcome: a raging river with a monstrous serpent, the desert where the abominable Sandman lives and the magician's wicked spells. However, Aladdin is fortunate to have things to help him, a magic lamp with a friendly genie and a magic carpet.

Illustrations © Pete Smith/Beehive Illustration.

Dear helper
Objective: To compose and write a story from a given plot.
Task: Read the story plot together and use the cards as prompts for discussion to help your child compose and write 'Aladdin's adventure' on a separate sheet of paper.

Name _____ Date _____

Choose the right word

■ Read the sentences and choose the right words to fill in the spaces. The first one has been done for you.

(park/car/jar)

Mandeep opened a **jar** of jam when he made some tarts.

(boy/toy/house)

Chelsea sat next to a _____ called James.

(good/brown/hood)

When it rained, Ben put the _____ of his coat over his head.

(June/July/March)

_____ is the month that comes before April.

(cow/joy/join)

Becky jumped for _____ when she won the swimming race.

(park/car/brown)

Joshua and Jade played on the swings in the _____ .

(joining/looking/shouting)

Ryan was looking forward to _____ the Cubs.

(part/far/wood)

Barnsley is not _____ from Sheffield.

(wood/now/out)

"Please take _____ your spelling books," said the teacher.

(took/good/march)

Hannah _____ her sister to the park.

Dear helper
Objective: To use awareness of grammar and context clues to predict missing words.
Task: Read the sentences with your child and look at the words in brackets. Try saying the sentences using each word and then ask your child to choose the right one and write it in the space provided.

Name _____   Date _____

Find the capitals

■ Look in your reading book and in other books, newspapers and magazines. Find words that begin with capital letters and write them down under one of the headings.

Beginning of a sentence	Name of a person	Name of a place	Name of day or month	Beginning of speech

Illustrations © Pete Smith/Beehive Illustration.

Dear helper
Objective: To revise knowledge about the use of capital letters.
Task: Explain to your child to look only for words that are printed in upper and lower case – that is, 'Megan', not 'MEGAN'. Headlines and titles are often printed in capital letters. You could talk with your child about why this is done: to make words stand out.

Name _____   Date _____

Find the compound words

■ Read the text and underline the compound words.

■ Write them in the table and write the two
words that make up each one.

Everyone was enjoying the sunshine. Everywhere you
looked you could see sunbathers. Some were reading
newspapers, some were sitting on deckchairs sleeping,
and some were building sandcastles.

　　Children played football or cricket. It was as if the
seaside was a giant playground. Instead of schoolteachers
on playground duty, there were lifeguards to make sure
everybody was safe.

compound word	words that make the compound word
	+
	+
	+
	+
	+
	+
	+
	+
	+
	+
	+
	+
	+

Illustrations © Pete Smith/Beehive Illustration.

Dear helper
Objective: To be able to split familiar compound words into their component parts.
Task: Read the text together and try to identify the compound words. Help your child to write the
compound words and their constituent parts.

Name   Date

Simon says!

Turn left.	Turn right.	Sit down.	Jump.
Stand still.	Turn around and face the opposite way.	Hop on your right foot.	Turn all the way round.
Touch your left knee with your right hand.	Touch your right foot with your right hand.	Touch your left ear with your right hand.	Put your left hand in the air.
Stand still.	Touch your right ear with your left hand.	Walk backwards five steps.	Walk forwards five steps.

What to do

1. Cut out the instruction cards. Use your scissors carefully.
2. Read the instructions on each card. If there are any you don't understand, talk about them with a helper.
3. Now turn the cards over and mix them up.
4. Choose six cards and hold them in your hand.
5. Read each one and perform the action.

Dear helper

Objective: To develop and reinforce knowledge of directions and instructions.

Task: If necessary, offer your child help in reading and understanding the instructions, but do encourage them to try to work out what should be done. If you wish, you could add some instruction cards of your own.

Illustrations © Pete Smith/Beehive Illustration.

PHOTOCOPIABLE **SCHOLASTIC**

www.scholastic.co.uk

Name	Date

Stick in the mud

🔳 Read the instructions and then explain to someone how to play the game.

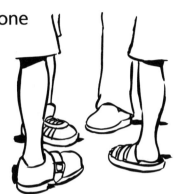

1. First decide who is going to be 'it'. You could do this by each putting a foot into a circle and asking one person to say a rhyme to decide. Here's one you could try:

   Mickey Mouse built a house underneath a tree
   Which number was it?
   One, two, three.

   One person touches each foot each time they say a word. The person whose foot is touched on the word three is 'it'.

2. The person who is 'it' counts to ten while everyone else runs away.
3. After counting to ten, 'it' can chase the others.
4. When 'it' touches (tigs) someone's back, that person has to stand still with legs apart.

5. If a player who has not been 'tigged' crawls through the legs of someone who has, that person is released and can run away again.
6. 'It' carries on until everyone has been 'tigged' and is standing still.

Illustrations © Pete Smith/Beehive Illustration.

Dear helper
Objective: To read simple instructions for a game, and to learn and recite favourite poems.
Task: Read the instructions with your child and then ask them to explain to you how to play the game. If possible, play the game with your child and others. You need at least three people to play. Talk about any rhymes you know that are used to decide who should go first.

Name

Date

Making a pancake

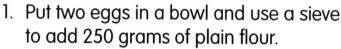

■ Read the instructions for the recipe. Then use the table to show which ingredients and utensils are needed.

1. Put two eggs in a bowl and use a sieve to add 250 grams of plain flour.
2. Add half a litre of milk and beat with a whisk until smooth and creamy.
3. Heat a knob of butter in a frying pan until it melts.
4. Pour enough of the batter into the pan to cover the surface and use a spatula to turn the pancake when it starts to set.
5. When both sides are golden brown, take the pan away from the heat and use the spatula to lift the pancake onto a plate.
6. Sprinkle the pancake with sugar and use a lemon squeezer to dribble lemon juice over it.
7. Take a knife and fork and enjoy eating your pancake.

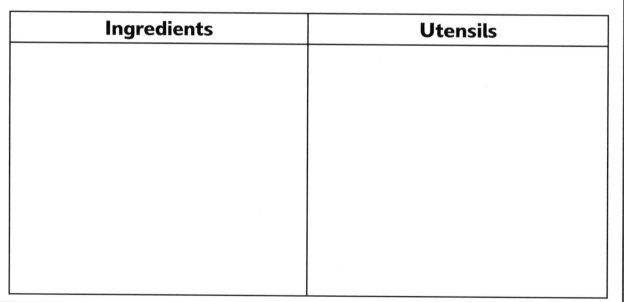

Ingredients	Utensils

Illustrations © Pete Smith/Beehive Illustration.

Dear helper
Objective: To read simple written instructions and to learn new words related to a particular topic.
Task: Talk with your child about ingredients and utensils. You could get out some items from your kitchen and ask your child physically to sort these into ingredients and utensils. Your child might indicate that scales and a measuring jug are needed to weigh the flour and measure the milk. If necessary, help your child to write the names of the ingredients and utensils in the boxes.

PHOTOCOPIABLE **SCHOLASTIC**
www.scholastic.co.uk

Name	Date

Reading instructions

◼ Read the instructions and look at the pictures. Then try to make the paper aeroplane.

Making a paper aeroplane

1.	Fold a piece of paper in half. 	5.	Fold each corner into the middle twice more. 
2.	Open the paper out. 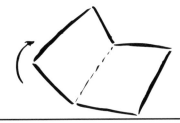	6.	Fold along the first crease so that the centre of the aeroplane sticks up. 
3.	Take one corner of the paper and fold it to the centre of the paper to where the crease is. 	7.	Fly your aeroplane by taking hold of the centre and throwing the plane upwards. 
4.	Do the same with the corner next to it. 		

NON-FICTION

Dear helper
Objective: To read and follow instructions.
Task: Look at the instructions together and ask your child to read them with you and to you. Make the paper aeroplane together.

Name	Date

NON-FICTION

Cleaning your teeth

Now brush your teeth, taking care to clean all of them.

When the brush is wet, take the toothpaste and squeeze the tube until you have covered the tips of the bristles with paste.

Next, put your toothbrush under the tap.

Finally, put your toothbrush and toothpaste away and dry your face.

First take your toothbrush and turn on the cold tap.

Remember to brush up and down.

Rinse your mouth with water and turn off the tap.

Instructions often begin with words such as:

first   next   then   after   that   when   finally

They also often begin with verbs that tell us what to do.

■ Read the instructions above, which are in the wrong order. Look at the first words in each sentence and then try to put the instructions into the right order. You don't need to write the instructions, just put the boxes in the right order.

Illustrations © Pete Smith/Beehive Illustration.

Dear helper
Objective: To develop and reinforce knowledge of instructions and to look at words that link sentences.
Task: Look at the instructions together and ask your child to read them with you and to you. Encourage them to experiment with arranging the order. When satisfied with the correct order, your child should stick the sentences down on a piece of paper.

PHOTOCOPIABLE ■SCHOLASTIC
www.scholastic.co.uk

Name   Date

Write your own instructions

■ Make a collection of instructions you can find around your home. For example, look for recipes and instructions for games.

■ In the box below, write down some of the words that begin sentences in instructions.

■ Now write some sentences that begin with the words you have found.

Illustrations © Pete Smith/Beehive Illustration.

NON-FICTION

Dear helper
Objective: To write simple instructions.
Task: Look at instructions with your child. Identify some of the words that begin instructions. Point out that these are often sequence words, such as *first, then, after,* or verbs that tell you what to do, such as *mix, place, move, cut.*

Name   Date

Hide and seek

◼ Look at the pictures and write instructions to go with each one to explain how to play hide and seek.

Illustrations © Pete Smith/Beehive Illustration.

NON-FICTION

Dear helper
Objective: To write simple instructions for a game.
Task: Look at the pictures with your child and help them to write instructions that are simple and clear.

Name	Date

Writing instructions

◼ Make a paper aeroplane.

◼ Now write instructions for making the aeroplane in the left-hand boxes below. Begin your sentences with words such as:

First   Next   Fold   Fly   Finally

◼ You might like to draw simple pictures in the right-hand boxes to illustrate each of the instructions.

◼ Ask someone to try making your paper aeroplane. If the person finds it easy to make the aeroplane, you have probably written good instructions!

Illustrations © Pete Smith/Beehive Illustration.

Dear helper
Objective: To write clear instructions and test them out.
Task: Ask your child to describe the process of making the aeroplane before writing it down. Ask questions such as: *What did you do first? Which way did you fold the paper? Does it matter if you do it this way or that way?*

NON-FICTION

Making compound words

■ How many compound words can you make using the words above? You may use each word as many times as you like. Write your compound words below.

every	bed	track	grand	cloth
father	one	room	table	suit
book	where	any	mother	case
motor	news	bath	bike	paper
tooth	hair	brush	no	paste

_____

_____

_____

_____

_____

_____

_____

Dear helper
Objective: To be able to build compound words using component parts.
Task: Read all of the words together. You might like to cut them out. Try different pairs of words next to each other and see if they make compound words. If in doubt, use a dictionary to check if the words you have made exist.

PHOTOCOPIABLE ▲SCHOLASTIC
www.scholastic.co.uk

How many syllables?

■ Look at the table below. Read the words in each column.

one syllable	two syllables	three syllables	four syllables
dog	rabbit	elephant	rhinoceros
Beth	Gopal	Oliver	Alexandra
York	London	Nottingham	Middlesborough

■ Now see if you can fill in all of the spaces with words that have the right number of syllables. You will probably find it easier to find words with one or two syllables than to think of words with three or four.

! **Tip:** You could look in an atlas or a newspaper for ideas.

Dear helper

Objective: To identify and count syllables in multisyllabic words and to note syllable boundaries in speech and writing.

Task: Remind your child about syllables by clapping the syllables in names and familiar objects. For example, *Liv-er-pool* has three syllables and would need three claps, while *pho-to-graph-y* has four and would need four claps. By developing an appreciation of syllable boundaries, your child should find it easier to break up difficult words when reading or spelling.

CORE SKILLS

Matching syllables

Monday	Tuesday	Wednesday	Thursday
Friday	Saturday	Sunday	January
February	March	April	May
June	July	August	September
October	November	December	one
two	three	four	five
six	seven	eight	nine
ten	eleven	twelve	thirteen
fourteen	fifteen	sixteen	seventeen
eighteen	nineteen	twenty	yellow
purple	blue	green	orange
Manchester	Liverpool	Newcastle	Bath

■ Cut out the words and spread them out so that you can see them all.

■ Put them into four groups:

   □ one-syllable words   □ two-syllable words

   □ three-syllable words   □ four-syllable word

Illustrations © Pete Smith/Beehive Illustration.

Dear helper

Objective: To identify and count syllables in words.

Task: Remind your child about syllables by clapping the syllables in names and familiar objects. For example, *Sept-em-ber* has three syllables and would need three claps, while *Febr-u-ar-y* has four and would need four claps. If your child finds the game easy, you could add some more words. You may wish to add some more four-syllable words.

Name   Date

Find out where

■ Answer the questions by looking carefully in the index below. Remember to use alphabetical order to find the word you are looking for.

All about pets: Index

B	budgerigars	9, 10
C	cats	15, 16
D	dogs	21, 22
F	fish	19, 20
G	gerbils	3, 4
	guinea pigs	2, 3
H	hamsters	1, 2
M	mice	4, 5
P	parrots	17, 18
S	snakes	23, 24

1. Which pages will you look at to find out about goldfish? _____

2. Which pages will tell you about a more dangerous pet? _____

3. Which pages will I look at if I would like a bird as a pet? _____

4. Which pages will tell me about pets that live in water? _____

5. Which pages will tell me about pets that have bright-coloured feathers? _____

NON-FICTION

Dear helper
Objective: To be able to find information from an index.
Task: Help your child to read each question carefully, and remind them to scan their eyes down the index to find the appropriate information.

Name	Date

Make an index

◗ An index is in alphabetical order with page numbers next to different items. Look carefully at the list of toys below.

◗ Put the toys into alphabetical order and write them with the page numbers (which are in brackets) in the grid below.

trains (2)	dolls (4, 5)	baby toys (31, 32)
outdoor toys (28, 29, 30)	jigsaws (15)	costumes (19)
paper aeroplanes (6)	board games (16, 17)	cars (22, 23)
model kits (12)	cards (18)	books (24, 25, 26)
computer games (9, 10, 11)	action figures (3)	sand toys (27)

Toy	Page numbers

◗ Check that your index is in alphabetical order.

Dear helper
Objective: To be able to make a short index in alphabetical order.
Task: Help your child to sort the names of the toys into alphabetical order and to write them in the grid, putting the page numbers in the right-hand column.

PHOTOCOPIABLE 📖SCHOLASTIC

www.scholastic.co.uk

Name   Date

How I do my shopping

■ In this flowchart the boxes are in the wrong order.
Cut them out and stick them onto a piece of paper
in the right order. Draw arrows between the boxes
to make a flowchart like this one.

> I go to the checkout.

> I pay for the things I have bought.

> I find a trolley.

> I put things in bags after the assistant has scanned them.

> I choose the food I want to buy.

> I go into the supermarket.

Illustrations © Pete Smith/Beehive Illustration.

NON-FICTION

Dear helper
Objective: To produce a simple flowchart that explains a process.
Task: Read the information in each box with your child and then cut out the boxes. Discuss the logical
order for the boxes and then help your child to stick the boxes onto a sheet of paper to produce a
flowchart similar to the one above.

Name   Date

How I made a bulb light up

■ The statements explaining how someone made a bulb light up are in the wrong order.

■ Cut them out and stick them onto another piece of paper in the right order.

Next I connected the other ends of the wires to each end of the battery to make a complete circuit.	A circuit is like a ring of metal for electricity to flow around.
I am going to explain how I made the bulb light up.	A break in the circuit would stop the flow of electricity.
When I had made a complete circuit by attaching the wires to the bulb and the battery, the bulb lit up.	Firstly I connected the wires to the metal part of the bulb.

Illustrations © Pete Smith/Beehive Illustration.

Dear helper
Objective: To understand how to explain a process.
Task: Support your child in sorting out the order of the explanation of how to make a bulb light up. Talk about the words that link together why and how as these give clues as to the correct order of the process.

Name	Date

How I grew a bean

- ◢ Imagine you have grown a bean.
- ◢ You have to tell your friend what you used and how you used them.
- ◢ Use the pictures to help you explain what you did and how you did it.
- ◢ Write what you did under the pictures.

Illustrations © Pete Smith/Beehive Illustration.

Dear helper

Objective: To compose simple text explaining how to plant and grow a bean.

Task: Ask your child to imagine what steps they would take if they wanted to grow a bean. If you can, plant and grow a bean with your child and talk about what you did, and most importantly how you did it, at each stage. Support your child in writing an explanation for each part of the process using the pictures as a guide.

Name   Date

Make your own flowchart

■ Choose a process for making something.

■ Fill in the boxes in the flowchart to show the order in which things should be done. Here is an example to help you.

| Put some newspaper on the floor. |

| Take another brush and polish your shoes until they shine. |

| Brush mud and dirt off your shoes. |

| Brush polish onto your shoes. |

| Put some polish on a brush. |

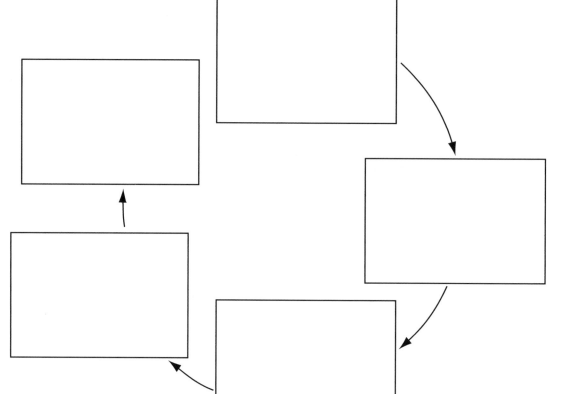

NON-FICTION

Illustrations © Pete Smith/Beehive Illustration.

Dear helper

Objective: To produce a simple flowchart that explains a process.

Task: Look at the sample flowchart together, then decide upon another process that could be explained using a flowchart. Discuss the logical order for the boxes and then ask your child to fill in the flowchart.

Match the meaning

◼ Look carefully at the lists of words. Draw a line
to connect the words that share the same meaning.
One has been done for you.

habitat	meat-eating
diet	dead
types	hunted animal
extinct	food
prey	kinds
hibernate	plant-eating
vegetarian	home
carnivorous	sleep through winter

Dear helper
Objective: To match words and phrases that express the same or similar meanings.
Task: Help your child to match the words to the correct meanings. You may like to help your child look
up some of the unfamiliar words in a dictionary.

Illustrations © Pete Smith/Beehive Illustration.

CORE SKILLS

Word sums

■ Look at the words below. They are all made by joining two words together.

■ Write the two words that make up each word in the space on the right. The first one has been done for you.

football   =   foot + ball

playground   =   _____

lawnmower   =   _____

dustbin   =   _____

postbox   =   _____

suitcase   =   _____

breadboard   =   _____

treetop   =   _____

hairbrush   =   _____

handbag   =   _____

toothbrush   =   _____

armchair   =   _____

Illustrations © Pete Smith/Beehive Illustration.

Dear helper
Objective: To split familiar compound words into their component parts.
Task: Compound words are words that are made up of two words joined together, for example *hair + brush = hairbrush*; *foot + ball = football*; *play + ground = playground*. Look at the compound words together and read them aloud together. Ask your child to try to find the two words that go together to make each compound word.

PHOTOCOPIABLE ■ SCHOLASTIC
www.scholastic.co.uk

CORE SKILLS

Words within words (1)

■ Look carefully at the words below. Find any words hidden inside them. Try mixing up the letters in each longer word to find other words. The first one has been started for you.

■ When you have finished finding words, check that you can spell the whole word correctly.

anything any, thing, thin, ant

happened _____

giant _____

managed _____

fortune _____

discover _____

frightened _____

careful _____

Illustrations © Pete Smith/Beehive Illustration.

Dear helper

Objective: To learn to spell unfamiliar words.

Task: This activity requires your child to look closely at the letters in each word, which will help them to remember how to spell them. Look first for words without jumbling the letters. If your child finds these quite easily, you can also try using the individual letters in the words to make further words.

Name

Date

NON-FICTION

The language of books

◼ Look carefully at the book cover and read the labels.

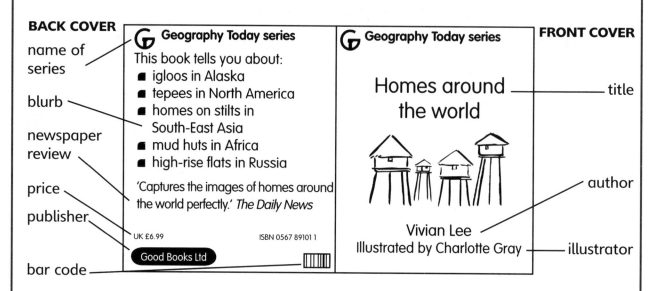

◼ Now write your definition of the words in the grid below.

What do the words mean?	
title	
author	
illustrator	
publisher	
blurb	
bar code	
price	

Dear helper
Objective: To be able to define words relating to book covers.
Task: Knowing the meaning of book-related words will help your child to talk about books more easily and to understand the information given on book covers. Look carefully at the picture of the book cover with your child and read the labels. Then help your child to write the meanings of the terms in the grid.

PHOTOCOPIABLE ◼SCHOLASTIC

www.scholastic.co.uk

Illustrations © Pete Smith/Beehive Illustration.

Name	Date

Find the telephone number

🔲 Look in a telephone directory at home, and see if you can find telephone numbers for people with these names.

Name	Telephone number
Williams, J	
Davies, M	
Smith, J	
Jones, S	
Andrews, R	
Gardner, N	
Baker, F	
Reed, J	
Arnold, T	
Barrett, P	
Knight, M	
Mathew, R	
Patel, M	
Evans, R	
Clark, L	
Fletcher, J	
Hall, M	
Powell, P	
Thompson, M	
Taylor, N	

Illustrations © Pete Smith/Beehive Illustration.

NON-FICTION

Dear helper

Objective: To be able to locate information in an index.

Task: A telephone directory is a type of alphabetical index. Help your child to practise alphabetical order skills and scanning for specific information by looking up these names in a telephone directory. They need to write the corresponding telephone number in the right-hand column. Don't worry if your directory doesn't have answers for all of these.

Name	Date

NON-FICTION

Cover story

◼ Look at these book covers. Then complete the grid below.

<table>
<tr>
<td>
This book tells you about:

◼ weather around the world
◼ blizzards
◼ hurricanes
◼ tornadoes
</td>
<td>
Weather

Ivor Storm

Illustrated by S K Y Blue
</td>
<td>
This book tells you about:

◼ 2D shapes
◼ 3D shapes
◼ making shapes
◼ shape patterns
</td>
<td>
Shapes

R U Square

Illustrated by P E N Tagon
</td>
</tr>
<tr>
<td>
This book tells you about:

◼ fashion through the ages
◼ fabrics
◼ designing clothes
◼ making clothes
</td>
<td>
Clothes

C L Rail

Illustrated by T Shirt
</td>
<td>
This book tells you about:

◼ ants
◼ beetles
◼ bees
◼ butterflies
◼ life cycles
</td>
<td>
Insects

A N Ant

Illustrated by Tony Beetle
</td>
</tr>
</table>

Name of book	Information contained
Clothes	
	number of body parts antennae feeding habits
Weather	
	cylinders, triangles making a pyramid repeating patterns

Illustrations © Pete Smith/Beehive Illustration.

Dear helper

Objective: To be able to find information from book covers.

Task: Look carefully at the book covers above and ask your child to read about what each book contains. Help your child to fill in the grid and encourage them to add extra ideas, based on the back cover information, when they are writing in the second column.

PHOTOCOPIABLE 📖 **SCHOLASTIC**

www.scholastic.co.uk

Name   Date

Noting the facts

■ Read the extract below about dinosaurs called maiasaurs.

■ Fill in the grid with notes about the key facts.

Maiasaurs

Maiasaurs were medium-sized dinosaurs that lived about 75 million years ago. Fossils have been found in the state of Montana in the United States of America. The fossils and other remains have told scientists a lot about maiasaurs. They lived in huge herds and were hunted by other dinosaurs, such as the tyrannosaurs. Maiasaurs ate a lot of leaves and plants and kept moving around to find food. Each mother laid about 24 eggs in her nest. A baby maiasaur weighed 1 kilogram when it was born and was about 35 centimetres long. When they were fully grown, they were up to 9 metres long and weighed approximately 2 tonnes, the same as four crocodiles.

	Facts about maiasaurs
Size when fully grown	
Weight when fully grown	
What they ate	
How the young were born	
What size they were when they were born	
Which country fossils have been found in	

Illustrations © Pete Smith/Beehive Illustration.

Dear helper
Objective: To be able to make notes from a non-fiction text.
Task: Help your child to read the extract all the way through first. Then support them in scanning the text carefully to find the particular information to put into the boxes.

NON-FICTION

Name   Date

Where does it belong?

■ Look at the list of words below. They need to be put in the correct sections of a catalogue. Write the words in the sections of the grid in alphabetical order.

hairdryers	jewellery	sofas	gloves	bicycle
shoes	footballs	washing	jigsaw puzzles	tables
pillows	slide	machines	school	high chairs
dolls	cots	dresses	uniforms	umbrellas

Accessories	
Baby equipment	
Children's clothes	
Electrical equipment	
Furniture	
Ladies' fashions	
Sports equipment	
Toys	

Illustrations © Pete Smith/Beehive Illustration.

Dear helper
Objective: To be able to match words to correct alphabetical sections.
Task: Look at the list of words and help your child to match them to the correct section, for example *washing machines* to *electrical equipment*. If there is more than one item for a section, help your child to put them into alphabetical order.

PHOTOCOPIABLE **SCHOLASTIC**
www.scholastic.co.uk

Name   Date

NON-FICTION

Write a dictionary page

◼ Look at the words and meanings below. The words have the wrong meanings. Match each word to its correct meaning and write them in the dictionary page. Make sure they are in alphabetical order. One has been done for you.

◼ See if you can add some of your own words.

Word	Meaning
excited	a bus that takes people on long journeys
water	a place by the sea
coach	costs a lot of money
check	something you drink that falls from the sky as rain
people	to make sure it is right
expensive	to feel very interested
travel	men, women and children
seaside	a short journey
trip	to go from one place to another

Word	Meaning
check	to make sure it is right

Dear helper
Objective: To be able to write a dictionary page of definitions.
Task: Help your child to write the words in alphabetical order and with corresponding definitions using the format above.

It's a match!

excited	expensive	coach
trip	people	water
travel	check	seaside
to feel very interested	costs a lot of money	a bus that takes people on long journeys
a short journey	men, women and children	something you drink that falls from the sky as rain
to go from one place to another	to make sure it is right	a place by the sea

- Read the words and meanings on the cards.
- Now cut the cards out.
- Play a pairs game with your helper, matching the word to its meaning. The winner is the one with the most cards at the end.

Illustrations © Pete Smith/Beehive Illustration.

Dear helper
Objective: To be able to match definitions to words.
Task: Help your child to read all the words and definitions carefully. Cut out the cards and play a pairs game. Turn the cards face down and spread them out. Take turns with your child to turn over two cards at a time. If they match, keep them. The winner is the person with the most pairs at the end.

Alphabetical order

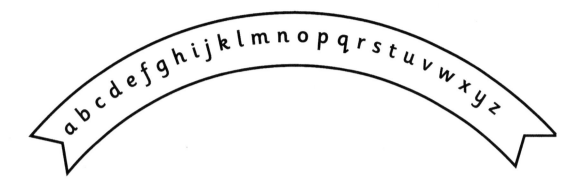

■ Look at the words in each group, then arrange them in alphabetical order. The first one has been done for you.

two	once	people	**once**	**people**	**two**
who	laugh	have	_____		
want	half	laugh	_____		
love	some	should	_____		
one	once	water	_____		
would	want	many	_____		
said	was	could	_____		
you	come	who	_____		
their	your	was	_____		
have	who	two	_____		

Dear helper
Objective: To be able to spell common irregular words and to develop understanding of alphabetical order.
Task: Read the groups of words together and help your child to arrange them in alphabetical order.

www.scholastic.co.uk

Punctuate the passage

▪ Read the text and then put in full stops and commas. Some of the words that begin with capital letters may help you.

Edith Howcraft

My grandmother is called Edith Howcroft She was born on 28th December 1900 She was nearly three years old when the first aeroplane flew As a little girl she hardly ever saw cars but she sometimes rode on a train The trains were pulled by steam engines which made a lot of noise and filled the air with smoke steam and soot

She went to school in a village two miles from her home She had to walk across fields to get to school and she had to walk back again at lunchtime because there were no school dinners in those days Her mother used to walk across the fields and meet her and her sister and they used to have picnics in the summer

When she was twelve my grandmother had to leave school and get a job She worked for a shopkeeper delivering meat bread fruit and vegetables She remembers falling off her bike and cutting her knee and losing all of the food one cold wet winter day

At Christmas the only presents my grandmother had were oranges nuts apples and home-made rag dolls She says that even though her family had very little money they were very happy and she would not change a thing about her childhood

Illustrations © Pete Smith/Beehive Illustration

Dear helper
Objective: To read for sense and punctuation.
Task: Read the text to your child and talk about it. Ask if anything is missing from the text. Talk about the way in which full stops tell us when sentences end and that one of the jobs of commas is to separate items in lists. Read the text with your child and ask them to tell you when full stops or commas might be included.

The question mark challenge

◼ Read the conversation between Hannah, who is three years old, and her mother. The computer has taken out all the question marks.

◼ Put the question marks in the correct places.

"What time are Aunty Wendy and Uncle David coming, Mummy"

"About 5 o'clock," said Mum.

"How long is that" asked Hannah.

"About two hours' time," replied Mum, trying to make the bed.

"I might be shy," said Hannah.

"Why" asked Mum. "You remember them, don't you"

Hannah was thoughtful for a moment, before asking another question. "What colour is their car" said Hannah.

"Blue," said Mum. "Now, stop asking questions."

"Why" said Hannah.

"Because I'm trying to get things done," said Mum.

"Why" said Hannah.

"Oh, stop saying 'Why'," said Mum.

"Why"

"Why are you called Hannah" replied Mum after a while.

"Because I am," said Hannah.

"Why is the world round, then"

"BECAUSE IT IS!" shouted Hannah.

"Now, can we get on" asked Mum.

Illustrations © Pete Smith/Beehive Illustration.

CORE SKILLS

Dear helper

Objective: To be able to punctuate questions correctly.

Task: Read the text with your child, encouraging plenty of expression. You may like to ask your child to read Hannah's part and you read the mother. Now see if you can help your child to put in all the missing question marks.

Adding '-ing'

Spelling **-ing** words can be tricky. Try to remember these rules:

Many words add **-ing** without any change of spelling:

shout → shout**ing**   laugh → laugh**ing**

Words ending in **e**, drop the **e** before adding **-ing**:

giggle → giggl**ing**   race → rac**ing**

Words with a short vowel before the last consonant, double the final consonant:

swim → swimm**ing**   win → winn**ing**

■ Add **-ing** to the verbs below. The first one has been done for you.

Word	Word +ing
clap	clapping
go	
hope	
jump	
like	
look	
pull	
ride	
rub	
say	
shop	
smile	
take	
try	
walk	
write	

Illustrations © Theresa Tibbetts/Beehive Illustration.

Dear helper
Objective: To understand how spellings of verbs may alter when '-ing' is added.
Task: Remind your child that a *verb* is an action word. Check that your child understands which rule applies to each word and has written the '-ing' word correctly.

Name   Date

NON-FICTION

Children's games

◼ Read 'Games past and present' with the support of your helper.

Games past and present

Introduction
Although Victorian outdoor games are different compared to the games children play now, they are alike in some interesting ways.

Football
Football is as popular today as it ever was but children today, unlike in Victorian times, would not be going to the butcher's asking for a pig's bladder to blow up for a football. You will find today's children playing with high-quality footballs. The excitement from playing the game is the same now as it was for Victorian children.

Street games
Street games such as hide and seek, skipping and tag remain popular with today's children but are now often played in children's own gardens or in parks because of the enormous increase in traffic and dangers on the streets. Victorian children running along paths pushing a hoop resembles today's children on their scooters where the joy of running along a path, whether on a street or in a park, is the same.

Marbles and other games
Marbles vary in popularity at different times. Every era has its fashions, be it marbles, conkers, yo-yos, swap cards or games consoles. Whilst the games are very different, they are similar because of the way in which they capture a child's imagination such that for a time no other activity is more important.

Conclusion
Some games change, new games are introduced, some games stay the same, but whatever the game, the children's interest, enjoyment and imagination are the reasons for a game's popularity.

1. What do you notice about the way in which the report is set out?

2. Does it matter in what order the sections 'Football', 'Street games' and 'Marbles' are arranged?

3. What sections need to stay where they are and why?

4. How do you know what each section is about and why is this easy to pick out?

5. Where does it tell you what the report is about?

Illustrations © Pete Smith/Beehive Illustration.

Dear helper
Objective: To understand the features of a report.
Task: Support your child in reading 'Games past and present'. Then use the questions to continue a discussion about the layout and the features of the text.

Name

Date

Birds in our garden

◼ Read 'Report on birds' and discuss it with your helper. Use the success criteria to help you decide whether this report is good, fair or poor by putting ticks in the boxes. We have started it for you.

Report on birds

Birds that are resident all year in Britain and that have been in our garden

Robin, blackbird, great tit, blue tit, long tailed tit, greenfinch, goldfinch, dunnock, house sparrow, wren. Some of them only visited our garden in winter.

Birds that visit Britain in summer and have been in our garden

Chiffchaff, swift, house martin, swallow.

Birds that visit Britain in winter and have been in our garden

Waxwing, redwing, fieldfare

Birds that have built nests in our garden

Blackbird

A blackbird built a nest in the hedge in the front garden. We were very worried about it as we live next to a busy road but the blackbird parents were very good and the four blackbird chicks were raised successfully.

   Another blackbird built her nest in the hedge in our back garden which we thought was a better place for a nest as it was in a much quieter and safer. Although she laid four eggs, only one baby blackbird hatched but the male and female blackbird made sure it was well fed and we watched it come out of its nest and eventually fly away safely.

Success criteria	Good	Fair	Poor
The title tells you what it's about.		✓	
The subheadings stand out.			
The information is easy to read.			
The information is easy to find.			
The title stands out.			
There are spaces between the sections.			

Illustrations © Pete Smith/Beehive Illustration.

Dear helper

Objective: To know how to assess the quality of a report.

Task: With your child, read 'Report on birds' and discuss how the report presents the information by using some of the criteria in the grid. Decide how well this report meets the criteria and add any other criteria you may have talked about in your discussion.

Name

Date

In the city

■ Read the report 'City living', looking carefully at the layout and how the report is presented.

■ Think what questions you might ask if you wanted someone else to assess the report. For example, a good question might be: **Does the title tell you what the report is about?**

■ Make a list of your questions.

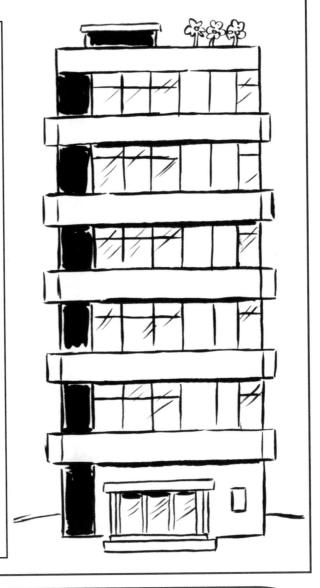

City living

High-rise
The tall thin design of a block of flats is ideal for housing a lot of people in cities and towns where there is often a shortage of space.

Gardens in the sky
On some blocks of flats the roof is made into a garden for growing such things as tomatoes and strawberries.

Wonderful views
People on the top floors have the advantage of being able to see amazing and wonderful views across the city.

Living in the sky
Flats provide an escape from the noise and bustle of the city streets below.

Illustrations © Pete Smith/Beehive Illustration.

Dear helper
Objective: To devise questions about a report.
Task: With your child, look at the report and discuss how the information is conveyed. Support your child in composing questions to be addressed by another child at school about the quality of the report. Prompts could include: whether the report is interesting; what makes it either easy or difficult to read; whether the subheadings stand out and so on.

Name

Date

My travels

- You are going to make a book about places you have travelled to.
- On a blank piece of paper, write down all the places you have travelled to.
- Next sort out the information into sections such as: places you have travelled to by train, school visits, family holidays, caravan holidays.
- Use the blank contents page to organise the sections of your book.

Contents

Introduction	Page 2
_____	Page _____
_____	Page _____
_____	Page _____
_____	Page _____
_____	Page _____
_____	Page _____
_____	Page _____
_____	Page _____
_____	Page _____
Index	Page _____

Illustrations © Pete Smith/Beehive Illustration.

Dear helper

Objective: To sort information into groups forming the sections for a contents page.

Task: Discuss with your child the places, transport, and reasons for their travels and capture this information on a blank piece of paper. Help your child to sort out the information into groups with common features in order to construct a contents page.

PHOTOCOPIABLE **■SCHOLASTIC**

www.scholastic.co.uk

Name	Date

Sports report

◀ Read the report.

◀ Divide the report into sections and cut out your sections.

◀ Lay out your sections of text on a separate piece of paper.

◀ Think of a good heading and subheading for each section.

◀ When you are happy with the layout and headings, stick all the pieces down.

Football is a team sport which is mainly played in the winter months. Footballers are often paid a great deal of money.

Football teams usually have 11 players a side and the games are played on grass pitches. Sometimes games are played with five players on each side and can be played on artificial pitches or in sports halls with smaller goals.

The main football competitions in this country are for the Premier League Championship and the F.A. Cup.

Cricket is a team sport played with 11 players on each team. Top cricketers are paid well but not usually as much as top footballers. Cricket is played in the summer months because the cricket ground and especially the wicket has to be dry, hard and even to have a good game.

The main cricket competitions in this country are the County Championship and the international competition for The Ashes between England and Australia.

Tennis is an individual sport or can be played by two people on each side. Tennis can be played all year round indoors but is usually played out of doors in summer. Tennis players can be very well paid.

The main tennis competition in this country is played at Wimbledon on grass tennis courts.

Illustrations © Pete Smith/Beehive Illustration.

Dear helper
Objective: To use headings and subheadings to show sections of different information.
Task: Read the report with your child and support your child in making decisions about separating the report into meaningful sections. Discuss the content of the report and encourage your child to decide upon a preferred heading with appropriate subheadings.

Name   Date

We need energy!

 Read the report 'Making electricity' and make notes so that you can tell a friend about it.

Making electricity

For many years we have relied on power stations that burn coal, gas or oil to provide the energy needed to produce the electricity we use in our homes. However, these resources are running out so we need to think of other ways in which we can make electricity.

Renewable sources of energy

Wind power, solar power from the sun and water power are renewable energy sources.

Wind power

Electricity is made by wind turning large blades, rather like large toy windmills, which then drive turbines to produce electricity. There can be many wind generators grouped together called wind farms.

Solar power

The sun's power can be made into electricity by solar panels which convert the sunshine into electricity.

Water power

The run of the river and the movement of waves can generate electricity.

Conclusion

There are several different ways of producing electricity, other than using traditional power stations. Energy to produce electricity can be made from sources that will not run out, called renewable sources.

Illustrations © Pete Smith/Beehive Illustration.

Dear helper
Objective: To make notes from a report.
Task: With your child read, the report 'Making electricity'. Discuss what the main points in the report are so that your child can produce a set of notes that capture these points.

PHOTOCOPIABLE **SCHOLASTIC**

www.scholastic.co.uk

Name   Date

All about birds

◼ Write a report from the notes about birds.

◼ Cut out the notes and think about how the information could be sorted to make different sections in your report.

◼ Think of a heading for your report that clearly tells someone else what it is about.

◼ Think of subheadings that are suitable for your separate sections.

◼ Start with an introduction that lets the reader know what you intend to say in your report.

Barn owls eat mice.

Barn owls screech.

Blackbirds eat worms.

Swallows eat insects.

Barn owls nest in barns.

Swallows nest under the eaves.

Blackbirds sing.

Swallows twitter.

Blackbirds nest in hedges.

Illustrations © Pete Smith/Beehive Illustration.

Dear helper
Objective: To write a report from notes.
Task: With your child, look at the notes and discuss what they tell you about the different birds. Ask your child how the information can be grouped in order to write a report. Support your child in choosing a heading for the report and in selecting suitable sections with appropriate subheadings.

A little snivel

■ Add **-el** or **-le** to each of the word beginnings below.

Word beginning	Add -el or -le	Word beginning	Add -el or -le
ab		lab	
barr		midd	
bott		mod	
cab		mudd	
cam		parc	
cand		possib	
circ		pudd	
cru		quarr	
doub		simp	
examp		squirr	
fu		tab	
gigg		terrib	
gosp		tow	
horrib		trav	
hot		tunn	
icic		unc	
jew		vow	
kenn		wobb	

Illustrations © Theresa Tibbetts/Beehive Illustration.

Dear helper
Objective: To learn and use the spelling patterns '-le' and '-el'.
Task: Encourage your child to say the word (by adding an 'l' sound to the word beginning) and then to choose one of the endings to write in the adjacent column.

Shopping game

potatoes	trainers	TV	guitar
pizza	socks	games console	pipe organ
bread	computer	DVD player	paintbrush
pasta	printer	CDs	hammer
jeans	keyboard	clarinet	pliers
T-shirt	mouse	cello	screwdriver

◼ What did you buy when you went shopping? To find out, cut out the cards, shuffle them, turn them face down and then pick out up to five cards.

◼ Write the items in a list like this:

> I bought a paintbrush, jeans, T-shirt **and** a mouse.

_____

_____

 Remember!
Use a comma after each item, but not before **and**.

Illustrations © Theresa Tibbetts/Beehive Illustration.

CORE SKILLS

Dear helper
Objective: To use commas to separate items in a list.
Task: Play this game with your child. Take it in turn to select cards and write lists. Add to the variety by making more object cards – cutting up an old catalogue is a good way to do this. Have fun by trying to explain what you plan to do with the items.

Adding '-s'

activities	cats	half	scarves
armies	cities	inches	shelves
babies	clocks	kisses	spies
berries	countries	knives	telephones
bodies	dishes	lamps	televisions
books	dogs	leaves	thieves
boxes	elves	loaves	trenches
bushes	enemies	pencils	waltzes
calves	foxes	pennies	watches
carpets	glasses	pictures	wolves

■ Cut out the word cards, then sort them into four groups to match the four ways of adding **s** listed below.

- ☐ Most words add **s** to make the plural: pack → pack**s**.
- ☐ Words that end in **s**, **ss**, **sh**, **ch**, **x** and **z**, add **es**: wish → wish**es**.
- ☐ Words ending in **y** change to **ies** if the **y** follows a consonant: belly → bell**ies**.
- ☐ Some words ending in **f** change the **f** to **ves**: self → sel**ves**.

Dear helper
Objective: To learn basic rules for changing the spelling of nouns when 's' is added.
Task: This is a simple sorting exercise to help your child investigate four of the most important changes to words when 's' is added. All the words are 'regular' – none are exceptions to the rules. Help your child to start the sorting exercise, then let them continue unaided.

CORE SKILLS

The silence of 'lamb'

■ Every word below contains one or more silent letters. Say each word aloud, clearly but naturally, and listen carefully to the sounds you can hear. Find the silent letters in each word and underline or highlight them.

■ Learn the spellings of these words, then test yourself with a partner or your helper.

February   lamb

argue   fought   Wednesday

        answer

bomb   gnat

                      guess   rhyme

       biscuit

calm   half

            knew   who   write

castle   knife

daughter

Dear helper

Objective: To investigate, spell and read words with silent letters.

Task: Help your child to find the silent letters, then help them to learn the words. Give your child a test, but make it fun, and don't expect them to learn all the words at once!

Name   Date

Hands

■ Read this poem about hands.

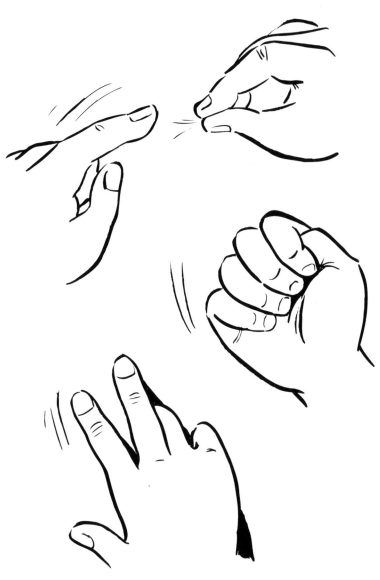

Hands
handling
dangling in water
making and shaking
slapping and clapping
warming and warning
hitting and fitting
grabbing and rubbing
peeling and feeling
taking and breaking
helping and giving
lifting
sifting sand
hand holding
hand.

Peter Young

Illustrations © Pete Smith/Beehive Illustration.

■ Lots of the verbs in the poem end with **-ing**. Think of some other verbs ending with **-ing** that show what hands can do. Write them on the back of this sheet.

■ Try writing your own poem using lots of **-ing** verbs to describe things which hands can do.

Dear helper
Objective: To read poems aloud and discuss them.
Task: Read the poem together and talk about it. Look at the verbs that end with '-ing' and talk about what they mean. Try writing a short poem together about what hands can do. Don't worry about making it rhyme. Concentrate on finding appropriate words (for example, *pinching, pointing, knocking, touching*) and using them.

Name	Date

I had a boat

◼ One of these of poems is a **rhyming** poem and the other is a **non-rhyming** poem. Say which is which, then look at the way they are set out.

I had a boat, and the boat had wings;
And I dreamed that we went flying
Over the heads of queens and kings,
Over the souls of dead and dying,
Up among the stars and the great white rings,
And where the Moon on her back is lying.

Mary Coleridge

My boat is my escape.
I push it out
onto the lake
and lie back
and look at the sky
and I feel I am
floating up there
far away
from my
problems.

Amy Reeves

Illustrations © Theresa Tibbetts/Beehive Illustration.

POETRY

Dear helper
Objective: To distinguish between rhyming and non-rhyming poetry and comment on layout.
Task: Your child will need most help with examining the way the poems are set out. Help them to look carefully at line indentations, punctuation, use of capital letters and so on. They should also read each poem aloud and think about the effect the line breaks have on the way the poem is read.

Name	Date

Homework poem

■ This homework poem is built up by repeating the first line and adding different excuses. Read the poem, then add some more excuses.

I didn't hand my homework in because
     I forgot it.
I didn't hand my homework in because
     I thought I had to hand it in tomorrow.
I didn't hand my homework in because
     it blew away on the way to school.
I didn't hand my homework in because
     my dog chewed it up.
I didn't hand my homework in because
     my mum couldn't do it.
I didn't hand my homework in because

I didn't hand my homework in because

I didn't hand my homework in because

I didn't hand my homework in because

I didn't hand my homework in because

■ On a separate piece of paper, write another poem based on repeated lines, for example:

I was late for school because…   The funniest thing I ever saw was…
      School dinners remind me of…

Illustrations © Theresa Tibbetts/Beehive Illustration.

Dear helper
Objective: To use repetitive phrases as the basis for writing poems.
Task: Help your child to brainstorm ideas for this poem and for their own poem. Discuss how to sort the ideas into the most effective order.

POETRY

Name   Date

Shapes with meaning

- Choose a special topic and write it in the centre of a sheet of paper.
- Write down your ideas around it as in the diagram below.

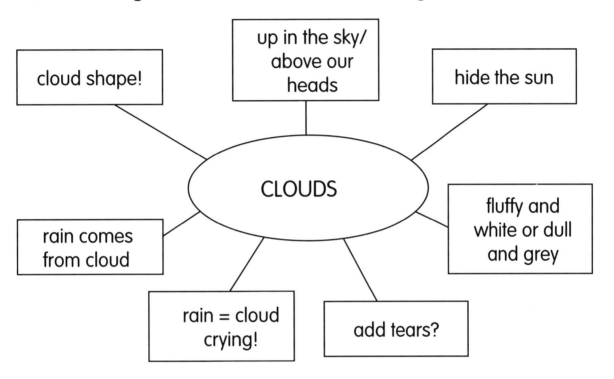

- Make decisions and choose what to include in your poem.
- The meaning of your poem should resemble the shape of your topic. Here is an example:

POETRY

Dear helper
Objective: To create a poem where the meaning is captured in the shape.
Task: Support your child by talking about a topic of their choice and collect their ideas as an ideas map as shown in the example. Discuss the words and pick out words and phrases to contribute to the poem, ensuring the discussion focuses on the pattern the words make as they are put together to convey the topic.

Months of the year

- Read the poem with a helper.
- Find the names of the months of the year.
Say them in order.
- Then turn the sheet over and write the months of
the year in order.

January brings the snow;
Makes the feet and fingers glow.

February brings the rain;
Thaws the frozen lake again.

March brings breezes loud and shrill,
Stirs the dancing daffodil.

April brings the primrose sweet,
Scatters daisies at our feet.

May brings flocks of pretty lambs,
Skipping by their fleecy dams*.

June brings tulips, lilies, roses;
Fills the children's hands with posies.

Hot July brings cooling showers,
Strawberries and gilly-flowers.

August brings the sheaves of corn,
Then the harvest home is borne.

Warm September brings the fruit,
Sportsmen then begin to shoot.

Fresh October brings the pheasant;
Then to gather nuts is pleasant.

Dull November brings the blast,
Then the leaves are falling fast.

Chill December brings the sleet,
Blazing fire and Christmas treat.

Sara Coleridge

*Dams are mothers.

CORE SKILLS

Illustrations © Pete Smith/Beehive Illustration.

Dear helper
Objective: To learn the sequence and spellings of the months of the year.
Task: Read the poem together and talk about what things the poet suggests each month brings. Ask your child to pick out the names of the months of the year. Then help them first to learn the names and then their spellings.

Words within words (2)

Jobs	Insects	Flowers
butcher	butterfly	bluebell
carpenter	daddy-long-legs	carnation
engineer	dragonfly	dandelion
fisherman	earwig	honeysuckle
programmer	grasshopper	rhododendron
Birds	**Fruit**	**Dogs**
kingfisher	blackcurrant	Airedale
moorhen	gooseberry	bloodhound
nightingale	orange	bulldog
partridge	peach	Dalmatian
puffin	pineapple	sheepdog
Geography	**Space**	**School**
capital	atmosphere	whiteboard
country	midnight	history
hillock	moon	mathematics
island	planet	poetry
plain	sunset	teacher

■ Cut out these cards, shuffle them, and then give two cards to each player.

■ Each player then has to see how many words they can find within the words on their cards.

Note: ❑ Consecutive letters only are allowed.

❑ The same word is only counted once (for example, three words on the **Birds** card contain **in**, but it can only be counted once).

Dear helper
Objective: To identify short words within longer words.
Task: Play this game several times with your child. Being able to identify short words within longer words is an aid to correct spelling.

Name   Date

Winter morning

Winter is the king of showmen,
Turning tree stumps into snowmen
And houses into birthday cakes
And spreading sugar over lakes.
Smooth and clean and frosty white,
The world looks good enough to bite.
That's the season to be young,
Catching snowflakes on your tongue.
Snow is snowy when it's snowing,
I'm sorry it's slushy when it's going.

Ogden Nash

POETRY

■ Read the poem together and then answer the questions.

1. What is the name of the poet who wrote 'Winter morning'?

    _____

2. Which word rhymes with **white** in the poem?

    _____

3. Which word rhymes with **snowing** in the poem?

    _____

4. Which word rhymes with **young** in the poem?

    _____

5. How does the poet describe snow when it is going?

    _____

6. Which line of the poem do you like best?

    _____

Poem © 1962, Ogden Nash (1962, Little Brown); illustrations © Pete Smith/Beehive Illustration.

Dear helper
Objective: To discuss poems using appropriate terms.
Task: Read the poem together and then talk about it. Look at it again and then help your child to answer the questions. You and your child may wish to write some sentences or lines of verse to describe winter.

PHOTOCOPIABLE ◨◨**SCHOLASTIC**
www.scholastic.co.uk

Name   Date

Noses

- Read the poem together.
- Find the sets of rhyming words. Write them down and discuss their different spellings.

I looked in the mirror
and looked at my nose:
it's the funniest thing,
the way it grows
stuck right out where all of it shows
with two little holes where the breathing goes.

I looked in the mirror
and saw in there
the end of my chin
and the start of my hair
and between there isn't much space to spare
with my nose, like a handle, sticking there.

If ever you want
to giggle and shout
and can't think of what
to do it about,
just look in the mirror and then, no doubt,
you'll see how funny YOUR nose sticks out!

Aileen Fisher

POETRY

Dear helper
Objective: To identify and discuss patterns of rhyme in a poem.
Task: Read the poem with your child. Talk about the groups of rhyming words and write them down on a separate sheet of paper. Look at the different ways in which the rhyming parts of the words may be spelled.

Name	Date

I only see middles

■ Read the poem with your helper and then read the poem by yourself.

■ Discuss what it is about, then practise reading the poem with expression.

Just now, I only see middles.
Middles of people,
Middles of cars,
Middles of checkouts.

Soon, I will see more than middles,

But not yet. Until then I will
Talk to my mum's coat,
Mix her up with someone else,
Hold hands with the wrong mum.

And, be told to look where I am going.

I DO!

Kathleen Taylor

Illustrations © Pete Smith/Beehive Illustration.

Dear helper
Objective: To read a poem with expression.
Task: Support your child in reading the poem by especially listening to the rhythms. Use the punctuation to help place the correct emphasis on the words and rhythm. This is to help your child practise and perform a poem.

Name	Date

Look, listen and feel

◀ With your helper, discuss the looks, sounds and feelings these pictures give and jot down words and phrases that come to mind.

◀ Choose something at home and draw a picture of it in the empty box and do the same.

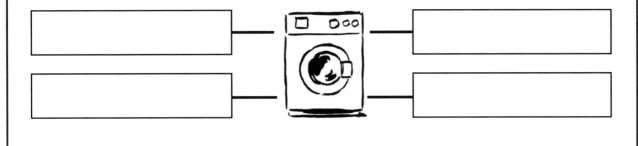

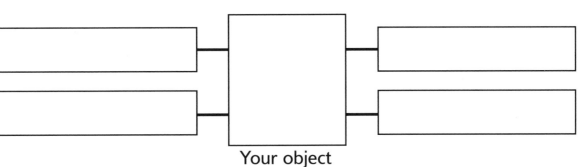

Your object

Illustrations © Pete Smith/Beehive Illustration.

Dear helper

Objective: To use a familiar object or home setting as a starting point for composing poetry.

Task: Use the pictures as a starting point for discussion and for generating words and phrases about them, but allow your child to choose something else that particularly interests them, such as a favourite pet or toy. Look at the real object if possible and draw your child's attention to the detail of what can be seen, the sounds it might make and how it makes you feel. Collect the words and phrases around a drawing of the object in the empty box. Your child will be using the collection of words and phrases to compose a poem at school.

POETRY

Cluttered desk

An important use of the **comma** is to divide up lists of words:

Example: I went to the shop and bought a box of cornflakes, a jar of jam,
a packet of tea, a loaf of bread and a tub of ice cream.

Notice that a comma is usually not required before the final item in a list because the word **and** is used to join the last item.

◼ Complete these sentences with lists based on what you can see in the picture. Don't forget to add **a** or **an** where needed and to use commas.

My desk was cluttered with

_____

_____

_____

For my birthday I'm hoping to get

_____

_____

_____

When I go to secondary school I will be studying

_____

_____

_____

In the toolbox there was

_____

_____

_____

Illustrations © Garry Davies.

CORE SKILLS

Long vowels

The grid below shows the most common ways in which **long vowels** are spelled.

◼ Look at the examples, then add your own in the third column.

a (ay)	Examples	Your examples
a	able	
ai	pain	
ay	day	
ey	prey	
e (ee)		
e	be	
ea	plea	
ee	see	
ei	ceiling	
ie	believe	
i (eye)		
i	idle	
ie	lie	
igh	high	
uy	guy	
y	spy	
o (oh)		
o	volcano	
oa	cocoa	
oe	foe	
ough	dough	
ow	blow	
u (you)		
ew	chew	
oo	too	
ugh	through	
ue	blue	

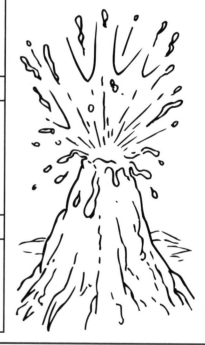

CORE SKILLS

Dear helper

Objective: To identify the long vowel sound in words and to see how the same sound may have different spellings.

Task: If necessary, remind your child that the vowels are 'a', 'e', 'i', 'o', 'u' (and sometimes 'y'). The long sound is the name of the letter.

Name   Date

Knock, knock

■ Read these 'Knock, knock' jokes.

■ Look at the way they are set out and discuss how they are similar to poems.

Knock, knock,
"Who's there?"
"Olive."
"Olive who?"
"Olive here, so let me in!"

Knock, knock,
"Who's there?"
"Frank."
"Frank who?"
"Frankenstein."

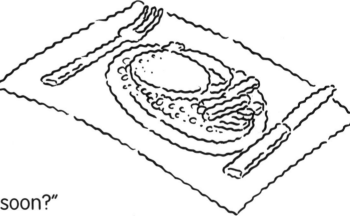

Knock, knock,
"Who's there?"
"Wilma."
"Wilma who?"
"Wilma supper be ready soon?"

■ Write some of your own 'Knock, knock' jokes on the back of this sheet.

POETRY

Illustrations © Theresa Tibbetts/Beehive Illustration.

Dear helper
Objective: To design simple patterns with words.
Task: Enjoy these 'Knock, knock' jokes with your child. Help them to think of other examples.

PHOTOCOPIABLE ■ SCHOLASTIC
www.scholastic.co.uk

Name	Date

Sandwich fillings

◾ Read this poem and talk about why it is funny. Think about another funny poem you know. How is it the same? How is it different?

◾ Write your own sandwich fillings poem on the back of this sheet.

Custard and sand,

Toothpaste and gravel,

Raw liver and clay,

Sawdust and candle grease,

Mousetails and mustard pickle,

Ashes and ice-cream,

Hamster bedding and vegetable oil,

Nuts, shells and ink,

Mouldy leaves and rats' ears,

Chalk dust and tree sap,

Squashed worms and washing-up liquid,

Dog food and bird seed,

Mushy banana and cement.

Anon

Extension

◾ Write a different kind of humorous poem or joke.

Illustrations © Pete Smith/Beehive Illustration.

POETRY

Dear helper

Objective: To discuss and compare forms or types of humour.

Task: Read the poem with your child, then discuss what makes it funny. Compare it with another humorous poem your child knows. Then compare it with other kinds of humour, such as 'Knock, knock' jokes and limericks. Together, think of various ways in which humour is created by writers. Discuss ideas for another sandwich fillings poem and, if appropriate, for another kind of humorous poem or joke.

Name	Date

What nonsense!

■ Read 'Little Miss Muffet' using the dots to help you tap out the beat.

■ Use the rhythm of the nursery rhyme and some of the words to help you write a new poem about a new silly character you have invented.

■ Choose silly words to complete your nonsense rhyme.

Little Miss Muffet

Little Miss Muffet

Sat on a tuffet

Eating her curds and whey

When down came a spider

Who sat down beside her

And frightened Miss Muffet away!

Pretty Miss Trippet

Pretty Miss Trippet

Danced on a bucket

Drinking her drippy glue

When _____ a _____

Who _____ her

And _____ Miss Trippet _____

Dear helper

Objective: To use a framework in order to write a nonsense poem.

Task: Read the nursery rhyme together and tap out the beat. The dots on top of the words give the beat. Then help your child to substitute some of the original words with words of their own, including a new name to fit the beat, for example *Thomas E Trifle* or *Pretty Miss Trippet*. We have started one poem with Pretty Miss Trippet as an example of how to proceed. It is important not to contrive the words but rather to support your child's choices. The chosen words can, and should be, invented to fit the rhythm rather than labour over trying to find real words.

Solomon Grundy

- Read the poem.

Solomon Grundy,
Born on Monday,
Named on Tuesday,
Married on Wednesday,
Took ill on Thursday,
Worse on Friday,
Died on Saturday,
Buried on Sunday.
That was the end
Of Solomon Grundy.

- Now look carefully at the days of the week:

Monday   Tuesday   Wednesday   Thursday
Friday   Saturday   Sunday

- Write the correct day for each of the questions below:

When did Solomon Grundy die? _____

When did Solomon Grundy get married? _____

When was Solomon Grundy born? _____

When did Solomon Grundy take ill? _____

When did Solomon Grundy get worse? _____

When was Solomon Grundy named? _____

When was Solomon Grundy buried? _____

- Do you think Solomon Grundy only lived for a week?

Dear helper
Objective: To learn to spell the names of the days of the week.
Task: Read the poem with your child and then do the activity together. Discuss the last question. Later, you may wish to help your child to learn the poem by heart.

CORE SKILLS

Alliterative sentences

◼ Look at the pictures of characters and read the list of names, adjectives and verbs.

◼ Write a silly sentence about each character with lots of words that have the same sound at the beginning. One has been done for you.

Characters	Adjectives	Verbs
Belinda the baby	beautiful	bawls
Winnie the witch	wicked	watches
Bill the burglar	beastly	bumps
Pete the pirate	perfect	paints
Fiona the fairy	funny	fusses
Tilly the teacher	tidy	taps

1. Belinda the beautiful baby bawls behind the building.

2. _____

3. _____

4. _____

5. _____

6. _____

Illustrations © Pete Smith/Beehive Illustration.

Dear helper
Objective: To be able to play with sounds in words to make particular effects.
Task: Look carefully at the pictures of the characters and then read the list of names, adjectives and verbs. Now help your child to put these together into sentences. It does not matter if they do not make sense. That makes them more fun!

Chefs and chiefs

The plural of most words ending in **f** or **fe** is formed by changing **f** or **fe** to **v** and adding **es**: for example **wife** → **wives**.

Learn these exceptions: **beliefs**, **chefs**, **chiefs**, **clefs**, **reefs**, **roofs**.

■ Complete the table by writing the plural forms.

Singular	Plural
belief	beliefs
calf	
chef	
chief	
clef	
dwarf	
elf	
half	
hoof	
knife	
leaf	
loaf	
reef	
roof	
safe	
scarf	
self	
sheaf	
shelf	
thief	
wharf	
wife	
wolf	

Illustrations © Garry Davies.

CORE SKILLS

Dear helper
Objective: To learn plural forms of words ending in '-f' or '-fe'.
Task: Help your child to memorise the list of exceptions to the spelling rule. Try making up a nonsense sentence to remember them. Here's one: *The chief chef stands on the roof and shouts his belief that the treble clef and a coral reef have much in common.* Check that your child does not forget them when completing the table.

Also available in this series:

ISBN 978-1407-10115-6

ISBN 978-1407-10116-3

ISBN 978-1407-10117-0

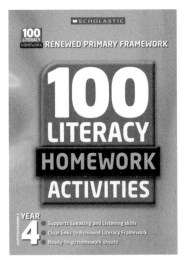

ISBN 978-1407-10118-7

ISBN 978-1407-10119-4

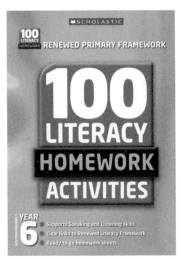

ISBN 978-1407-10120-0

To find out more, call: 0845 603 9091
or visit our website www.scholastic.co.uk